JEFFREY SHAW

LING*

DISCOVER YOUR IDEAL CUSTOMER'S
SECRET LANGUAGE AND MAKE YOUR
BUSINESS IRRESISTIBLE

Creative Warriors Press

This book is dedicated to my three children: Connor, Clare and Lillian, who taught me everything I know about the most important communication of all: How to speak to their individuality and listen to their infinite wisdom. I'm hoping this book will give them something more than my waffles to remember me by.

CONTENTS

INTRODUCTION

STANDING TO ONE SIDE OF the velvet rope, I waited my turn to see the bank teller. I had one goal for the day: to transfer my "salary" from my business account to my personal account. Shifting my weight from one foot to another, I looked over the account transfer form for the third time. My eyes darted nervously from the form to the velvet rope, then back to the form again. I touched the rope. Wow, it really is velvet.

I've heard it said that money reveals truths. I suppose that's true, because every time I went to the bank, I felt as though I was about to find out if I was really the person I thought I was. I felt successful. I was told to fake it until I made it and, boy, was I faking it like a pro. But the bank teller had the power to tell me whether I really "made it." At twenty-three years old, "making it" was determined by how much money I earned. That determined how I felt about myself. Heck, it determined if I would make it through the weekend. Would they move the velvet rope and let me inside? Or would I be shut out?

When it was finally my turn to step up to the bank teller, tiny beads of perspiration appeared on my neck and hairline. I handed the teller the transfer form and tried not to look nervous as she checked my account balance.

"I'm sorry, there aren't enough funds available to make this transfer," she said. Ugh. Those dreadful words. The words I feared the most. The words that said to me, you're not who you think you are. You're a fraud. An imposter. You should just give up.

This was more than thirty years ago, and the amount I wanted to transfer was one hundred and fifty dollars. Yes, I didn't even have one hundred and fifty dollars from my business to pay myself. I had been working for three years as a portrait photographer and I was barely earning a living. That day at the bank, I couldn't even say I was getting by. I didn't have enough customers, and the customers I did have were not the right customers. I was all too aware of that fact, but I had no clue how to change it.

I am not the only entrepreneur with a similar story. Many of us experience this on a regular, if not constant, basis: working every day, rarely getting a break, and yet still not making ends meet, feeling as though we are imposters in our own industries, in our communities, in our own businesses. We're on the hamster wheel, running like mad with a tickertape of self-defeating thoughts running through our minds:

What am I doing wrong that I can't seem to get the right customers? Or any customers?

I'm just not any good at sales. Why am I such a hot mess?

Is there just no market for what I do? I'm not good at the business side.

We think the problem is us—the creative entrepreneurs, the innovators, the out-of-the-box thinkers. We just don't know enough about business, or we aren't good at networking, or there's something wrong with our product or service. And we've tried everything we can think of to build our customer bases and increase revenues, everything the marketing and branding experts tell us to do. We've tried to personalize our branding and our offerings by creating customer avatars and profiles. We've followed the cookie-cutter, transactional business practices. We work harder and try to work smarter and yet somehow we still end up behind the velvet rope, waiting to be told we don't have enough funds to pay ourselves.

I spent my first three years in business spinning on the hamster wheel. That day in the bank was a turning point. I had to get off that hamster wheel, stop working so hard and getting nowhere. I'd been trying to reach one type of customer, and my efforts just weren't clicking. I wasn't sure how to change my business practices, but I knew I had to do it.

After a conversation with a prospective customer—which I'll share in Chapter 1—I finally realized we weren't speaking the same language. I began to study the people and communities I wanted to serve. I paid close attention to how they communicated, their values and beliefs, their daily practices, their aesthetics, their way of life. I learned the "secret language" of my ideal customers—their lingo. I became so fluent in their lingo that I was able to forge an almost-instant connection with the customers I wanted. Within a year, my business increased fivefold. It wasn't long before I was one of the highest-earning portrait photographers in the country.

The truth is, you don't have to work that hard to find customers. In reality, a world of customers is waiting for you to show up.

Read that again. A world of customers is waiting for you to show up.

Understanding your customer's secret language allows you to establish a connection so genuine and authentic that the people you want to work with are simply drawn to you. They will end up at the doorstep of your business, waiting to be served.

Lingo is defined as "the language and speech, especially the jargon, of a particular field, group, or individual." Tribes, communities, and people of similar ilk all share a lingo. Speaking a common lingo is a way to bond and differentiate yourself within a community and separate yourself from the masses. It's a way to communicate that makes you feel as though you belong to a particular group. Bands such as The Grateful Dead wearing their tie-dyed shirts and designating their most loyal fans as tapers have been doing this for decades. Pop stars such as Lady Gaga and her Little Monsters share a lingo with the claw hand-gesture. Brands like MINI Cooper and Harley-Davidson have special waves for drivers as they pass one another. Trust me. There are YouTube videos explaining the nuances of perfecting "the wave." These are all part of a lingo, all an effort to bond, to show kinship, and to acknowledge that you are "one of them," that we are in this together.

That's the power of a lingo. That's not to say you have to create a repertoire of words or come up with a secret handshake. I mean, you can if you want to. But this is about understanding the lingo that's already there. A lingo speaks directly to the heart. To speak another person's lingo, you need to understand what makes them tick—their essence. Speaking someone's lingo touches them in unspoken ways, the way friends know you so well they know just what to say or do for you. To speak the lingo of the customers that you would most like to work with, you need to know how they think, what attracts them, and what makes them feel as if they belong—that they belong doing business with you and no one else.

Have you read *The 5 Love Languages* by Gary Chapman? The five love languages are words of affirmation, acts of service, physical touch, gifts, and quality time. Chapman says that people tend to feel loved in response to one of those five languages, or ways of expressing love. When I read the book, I was married and had three kids. When I applied Chapman's findings, I found that each member of my family of five represented one of the love languages. I needed to speak differently to each of my kids. What felt like love was different for each of them. This got me thinking, even then, about the power of speaking someone's language. It's really no different in business. It's not that you are going to speak a different language for each customer, but that every market—high-end, low-end, luxury, budget, and everything in between, has its own language, a language that customers in that market respond to, that, you could say, makes them feel loved.

Understanding this, you have the power to create the business you want and to work with the customers who are a pleasure to work with, who value what you do, and who pay you what you're worth. You can compel them, influence their buying decisions, and turn them into loyal followers and engaged advocates, all by understanding their lingo and speaking their secret language.

Make no mistake. There is nothing conniving, clever, or underhanded about knowing someone's secret language. In fact, I can hardly think of anything more generous than getting to know someone so deeply that you understand their lingo: what's compelling to them, what speaks to their heart, and what leaves customers with a profound sense that you "get them." To feel seen and heard are two fundamental human needs. Truly, is there any more satisfying feeling to fulfill those two needs?

The days of avatars, buyer personas, and demographics are gone. Today's customers require you to know more than their stats, more than their behavior. They want to sense that you get them. They don't want to be targeted; they want to be compelled. In order for you to be successful today, customers must feel aligned with your mission, feel you fully get them and they get you. Your clear brand message and image must cut through the noise so that your ideal customer finds you. You must stand out as uniquely qualified to serve them or provide the product they need.

With the Secret Language System laid out in this book, you will carve out your unique space in your chosen market. No need to worry about competition. There's plenty of room in any chosen industry for all to succeed.

Again, a world of customers is waiting for you to show up.

Gone are the days of hunting down and finding customers. Forcing yourself and your marketing on people is guaranteed to repel the very people you are trying to reach. Treating people as if they are one in a million will get you nowhere. People want to be made to feel as if they are THE ONE, even if they know it's in a million. And you know what? They deserve that. You are also a consumer and you deserve that too.

So, yes, the people you want to serve are already there waiting for you to show up. If you do the work to get to know their secret language with integrity, free of assumptions and judgements, they simply start finding you. *Field of Dreams* was a great movie, but I've always thought it gave terrible business advice. A business that thinks "just build it and they will come" is in for a rude awakening. However, in this case, if you build a business that speaks the secret language of the people you want to reach and get your business out there in an actionable way, they do come.

The bar has been raised. Good enough is no longer enough. Building businesses, offering your wares, and expecting people to buy will no longer work. Consumers expect more—closer relationships, more transparency, more authenticity. To succeed, we need to shift from transactional thinking to relational thinking at even deeper levels. We have to up our game.

Putting in the effort and getting to know the people you want to serve is one of the greatest acts of generosity I know of! Getting to know what makes people, tick, their behavior, and what triggers them should come from a place of true empathy with the intent to serve. I mean, seriously, don't we all want people in our lives who know us that well? Who seem like they are always a step ahead? Who perhaps know what we want before we do? Just thinking about it fills my heart. Imagine the impact you can have on the lives of your customers. You can think of it like learning a foreign language. Unless you're involved in some covert operations, we learn a foreign language in order to communicate better, to be more in the culture and lifestyle of those we want to communicate with, to have a better understanding, and, in a way, say, "I want to be one of you and part of your life and culture." The same can be said for understanding your ideal customer's lingo.

By the time you finish the book, you will have all that you need to connect with the right customers, get paid what you're worth, and have the business you've always wanted. It may not happen overnight, but will likely happen faster than you might think. Regardless of where you are today, there's a good chance I was where you are now.

You can do this. It doesn't matter what market you're serving—high-end or low-end—or where you're based geographically. You can make the Secret Language System work for you. Then you can be part of the movement that started with my podcast, Creative Warriors—those in business who want to make an impact, share their talents and passions, and make the world a better place by the creating deeper connections with those they serve. So let's get to it.

WHAT I REALLY WANT IS TO CHANGE YOUR LIFE

As MUCH AS I WANT to help you change your business for the better, what I really want is to change your life. Changing your business may, in fact, change your life. And changing your life will likely change your business. They go hand-in-hand. That's why, when writing *LINGO*, I set out to create a different kind of business book. You could say an "uncommon" business book for the uncommon entrepreneur.

In our world we are often put into boxes or in this case, a category. In the process of setting up and publishing a book, you are repeatedly asked, "Is it a business book?" "Is it a self-help book?" Pick a category was the instruction. As is often the case in our black-and-white world, we are forced to choose, and I'm left feeling like I want a third choice. Or better yet, I want it all.

I'll share a funny story and a way you might want to test how uncomfortable people are when you refuse to choose. I was once at a casual restaurant, just a couple blocks away from my home. It's a burger and fish sandwich joint, but I go for the fries. I can't turn down a good french fry. Per standard protocol, the waitress arrived at our table to take our order. My decision was a fish sandwich. She asked what kind of fries I wanted with my sandwich. "What are my choices?" I inquired.

She rattled off a litany of choices—curly fries, waffle fries, spicy fries, french fries, steak fries.

Mind you, I knew the choices because I've tried every one. So I said, "Yes!"

To which she responded, "Which one?"

"I'd like all of them, please."

"Sir," she said, "that would be a lot of fries."

"Oh, no," I explained. "I just want the normal amount of fries, but a sample of all of them."

"We can't do that."

"But why? I'm not asking for more than my fair share. I just want everything."

"We can't do that."

I knew I was starting to rattle her cage, getting her out of her comfort zone, I wanted to boost her up. So I said, "I'll bet you can if you try!"

She walked away, noticeably confused and probably thinking, "I wish this guy would move back to New York." Shortly thereafter, though, she arrived, rather amused, with my sandwich and a plate of all the different types of fries. I think she was proud of her accomplishment. What I hoped for was that she learned a lesson, that sometimes by refusing to choose between things, we are actually choosing to have everything.

In writing *LINGO*, I refused to choose between making it a business book or a self-help book. We need a third category. Because the truth is, my ideal customer, you, the reader, is speaking the language of business success and personal fulfillment. You don't just want a successful business. You also want to live the life you want. Paradoxically, the way to have everything, the successful business and fulfilled life, is to understand that it takes personal development to gain the success we want as well as smart strategy to move forward. Your success and personal development are strongly intertwined, and we need to resist a world that is constantly forcing us to choose. I want you to have everything. That's why *LINGO* is a unique business book.

In *LINGO*, you're going to read about how I came to understand the idea of a secret language between business and customer. It's a crazy story: how I instantly figured out the missing link as to why my business was failing. Then, within three months, I completely changed my business, started over with a whole new approach, and within a year multiplied my sales by five times. It may not be overnight, but that's a rapid change to go from gaining an understanding to significant results. And if you're a startup, well, what you'll learn in *LINGO* will save you years of struggle, if not make the difference between failure and success.

Once you understand the concept of secret Language, you'll learn the 5 Steps of the Secret Language Strategy. Each step is carefully explained so that you can implement the strategies on your own. Once you've learned how to build your business using the Secret Language Strategy, you'll move on to learning how to directly apply the Secret Language Strategy so you can expand and create maximum impact through your business.

LINGO wraps up in a unique way, which warrants explanation. I didn't want *LINGO* to be just another business book full of action steps. I've come to know that you can apply all the strategies, yet not get to where you want to go. You might gain some momentum but not feel fulfilled or be working really hard but hardly getting ahead. Along with the action steps and strategies, you need two other things:

1. Unblock whatever is in your way. You've heard people say they are their own biggest obstacle? It's very often true, and I'm going to help you get out of your own way.
2. Create a positive inward flow. You know how difficult it can be to receive? Or how we focus on one negative thing that is said and ignore ten positive ones? I'm going to help you instill daily practices to break this cycle.

The last section of *LINGO* is about mindsets and daily practices—not what you expect to find in a business book. But hey, you want everything, remember? You don't have to choose between business success and personal fulfillment. You've smartly chosen a book that will show you the path to both, because I refused to choose too.

I hope you find *LINGO* to be speaking your language. It was written just for you.

⊛CH. 1
THE SECRET LANGUAGE STRATEGY

IN AN IDEAL WORLD, BEING an entrepreneur would be easy. We would come up with a great idea, everyone would think we're a genius, and people would flock to our door and throw money at us. We would be proud of what we created and thrilled we are getting fairly compensated. Heck, more than fairly compensated. We would be getting rich! And the people buying our product or services would be the bomb—people we love to do business with, who bring us joy, and who are eager to spread the word about our awesomeness. Sounds great, right? Too good to be true? Maybe not.

This is an idealized version of my experience as an entrepreneur once I figured out what I'm going to share with you in this book. The concept of *LINGO* and the associated strategies have the potential to rock your world, help you build an amazing business or dramatically change the one you have, and make being in business so much easier than you ever imagined. Easy, you say? Yes, it can be much easier than you might expect. Instead of effort, it will take strategy.

Think about the difference between effort and strategy. As entrepreneurs, we are conditioned to put in a lot of effort: Be all in, never give up, hustle your way through. I'm not taking anything away from hard work. It does take hard work to get a business off the ground and survive the tumultuous world of being an entrepreneur. But at some time, you're likely to get the idea to work smarter, not harder.

But what exactly does that mean? To most people, working smarter means being more efficient, putting your effort where you're likely to get the best return. Again, an intelligent decision. But instead of all this effort and efficiency, what if you applied a strategy? A strategy is defined as a plan or method to obtain a desired goal, a thoroughly thought-through, step-by-step plan to get you the results you want.

So what do I suggest your strategy should be to make being in business easier, more profitable, and fulfilling? Work with the most desired customers, the customers who are best for your business, your "ideal customers." And how do you find said "ideal customers?"

First of all, you don't. They find you. See, isn't being in business getting easier already? Can you imagine a business where you're not hunting down customers and they are showing up at your proverbial doorstep eager to do business? A business where you finally realize that it's not your job to convince people of your value or the value of your product, where rather, it's your job to be sure you're found by the people who already value what you do.

The best strategy I know of to attract your ideal customers is to speak their language. To share a lingo. A lingo is meant to be just that—shared between you and me, us and them, your business and your ideal customers. Sharing a lingo creates a bond, and that bond not only helps your ideal customers find you, it helps you keep them.

WRONG FISH, WRONG POND

I STARTED MY FIRST BUSINESS in 1985. I was twenty and fresh out of photography school. Setting up shop in my small hometown about two hours north of New York City, I was determined to become a big fish in a small pond and make my father proud. To do that, I decided I would open a "high-end" portrait studio. I had it all planned out, right down to the pricing. A single 8x10 photo would cost $48.02. Yes, $48.02. Weird number, right? I came up with that number because we learned a pricing formula in photography school that I followed verbatim. But I assure you, for my hometown, $48.02 was a lot of money to charge for an 8x10 photo.

The area I grew up in was accustomed to high-volume, low-price photography studios like Sears and a chain called Olan Mills. But I believed that portrait photography was very important and I wanted their portraits to be important to my customers. I was going to create something no one expected, something that would be worth my higher price. Mistake number one. It was a mistake because it's a losing battle to try to convince someone to value anything they don't already value. That's "selling." When your customers already value your product or service, you don't have to "sell."

I set my sales goals for that first year, motivated by the opportunity to impress my father with not only meeting my goals, but crushing them. My goal was to earn thirty-six thousand dollars in the first year. When I landed a twenty-five-thousand-dollar catalog job, I was so excited. This was the big time, and I was only twenty years old! But, shortly after the catalogs began appearing in mailboxes, the company closed and stiffed me for the twenty thousand dollars they still owed me. I was devastated. But I recovered and was sharing my success with my father.

Then, just one month short of my first year in business, the unthinkable happened. Hours before my wedding, my father had two massive heart attacks and died in the ambulance on the way to the hospital. I can't quite put into words the impact. My heart and soul had been going in one direction, and suddenly life had a very different plan. Right away, an alarming thought occurred to me. It was a lesson I have lived with every day of my life since, and I encourage every entrepreneur to consider. Because of all my excessive hard work to start my business, I knew I was emotionally and physically in a very vulnerable state and not prepared to handle such a loss—not that anyone ever is, not completely. But to stretch yourself so thin, push your physical and mental state to the limits, thinking "I just have to get through the wedding" or to whatever imaginary deadline you might set, is a very dangerous way to live life. Yet so many of us do. We're constantly pushing forward. But if anything goes awry, we're not prepared.

The following two years cannot be described as anything short of pure hell. Not being physically and mentally capable of handling the loss of my father after having worn myself so thin put me into a cycle of anxiety and panic attacks, which needed to be medicated to get them under control. Panic attacks closely emulate a heart attack, so each attack only increased the fear of dying from a heart attack as my father had. It was a vicious cycle.

I could say my business suffered, but I don't know that it would have mattered if I could have been fully present. The truth was, there was very little business coming in. Convinced that a more upscale location would do the trick, I changed locations, which increased my expenses. It didn't. I had to come to terms with the fact that after three years of working really hard and overcoming huge obstacles, I was failing. It wouldn't be long before I had to give up.

One day, a lady came into my studio, and I made my very best pitch about the value of family photographs and the importance of handing down memories from one generation to another.

She looked at me and said, "I'm not sure how I'm going to pay my rent. I don't have the luxury of worrying about my children's memories."

In that moment, I realized I had been barking up the wrong tree. I finally understood why I was struggling, why my business was failing, why it seemed as though I was trying to move heaven and earth in the wrong direction.

I was the wrong fish swimming in the wrong pond. Most people have a brilliant idea and build a business the way they want it to be, then they spend their energy and time trying to find customers who fit that business. That's what I'd done. My idea might have been right, but I wasn't offering anything my potential customers wanted.

I was trying to sell something to someone who couldn't afford it. And probably offering what she didn't really want even if she could afford it! I was trying to sell the idea that a portrait is important for your children and for generations to come. But such long-term thinking was of little value to someone trying to scrape by day to day. We were completely misaligned, as if there was a pseudo-professional interchange between us but no real connection. I was being professional and she was, well, being herself. We began as complete strangers, and that's how we stayed. But something told me it didn't have to be that way. I didn't understand her or her needs at all. And she didn't understand me. Yet, I was trying to "sell" her something. No wonder it felt like moving heaven and earth. I mean, really, who the hell wants to be in the position to sell anything? There has to be a better way. I didn't know what that better way was, but I suspected there was one.

Of course, she left. I went into my camera room where it was dark and sat on the floor. I was done. Spent. After three years of fighting to get this business off the ground and working through my father's death, panic attacks, and the start of a marriage, I couldn't even pay myself a salary. I realized that I had made a huge mistake. I had built the business I wanted— my dream—where I wanted it, and attempted to impose it on the community in which I worked. I'd never asked a single person whether they wanted what I had to offer. I'd never considered whether the people there would value what I had to offer. I built the business I wanted before getting to know the people I was going to serve.

Huge mistake, yet one that is made every day. Entrepreneurs who are all fired up by their ideas and go-big-or-go-home motivational talks build the businesses they want before understanding those they want to impact and serve.

There had to be a better way.

The right way to build a business is what I call customer-centric: Define your ideal customers first and build a business that speaks to them.

UNDERSTANDING THE PEOPLE WHO I WANT TO SERVE

I HAD BUILT MY BUSINESS without understanding the market I was in. In actuality, I had built it backwards. The luxury product I was offering did not align with the lower socio-economic scale and values of my market. I needed to start over. I wondered what market would match my values for longevity and quality and realized my cash-strapped customer had provided the answer: those who can afford luxury—the affluent market.

There was just one problem. My only understanding of the affluent market came from watching Bing Crosby's Christmas specials on TV as a kid. Unlike my own lower-middle-class family, those people seemed to enjoy sitting around the fireplace together, wearing nice sweaters, and singing songs. I knew I had to learn a lot to serve the affluent market.

I decided I could educate myself about the lifestyle of the affluent by visiting high-end stores. So I made the two-hour trek to the one store I had heard about that was high-end: Bergdorf Goodman on Fifth Avenue in Manhattan. Bergdorf Goodman is a one-of-a-kind department store that caters to an exclusive customer. As exceptional as the store window displays are, many visitors to New York City pass right by the exquisite storefront and never realize it's there. Let's just say it's not meant for everyone.

When I entered Bergdorf Goodman through the revolving doors in my far-too-casual pants, a doorman greeted me. I may as well have landed on a different planet. What was this place with its crystal chandeliers, warm, subtle lighting, and impeccably dressed clerks? It certainly didn't have the fluorescent lights and blue light specials

I was accustomed to! As I stepped forward, a strange tapping noise interrupted the dignified low hum of the place. I realized it was a metal plate that had come through my shoe when the soles wore out. I had never walked on marble.

I meandered down hallways, occasionally stepping into small rooms and alcoves. I suspected the seventh floor, Decorative Home, would have some small, decorative item or accessory that I could afford with the twenty bucks I had to spend. Twenty dollars didn't go very far in a store like this, even in 1987. But I had an objective: I wanted to understand the lifestyle of the rich and famous. Specifically, what happened when they went shopping.

The only thing I could afford was a tiny votive candle. I asked for the candle to be gift-wrapped. The very nice sales lady—I hoped she thought I was the rich heir who could get away with being inappropriately dressed—walked me to the gift wrap department. I was introduced to a woman on the other side of an opening in the wall who, I was assured, would help me from there. Thinking this was someone I could relate to, I leaned forward through the opening in the wall and said, "Excuse me. I'm trying to learn how to make something look and feel expensive. Can you show me how to wrap this?"

With a slight grin and a wave of her hand, she invited me into her back room. She showed me how to wrap the candle in an abundance of tissue paper. Wads of tissue paper! She stopped and looked up at me as if to say the most important thing that I needed to hear.

"Don't use any tape," she said with conviction far greater than the point seemed to warrant. Coming from a family that wrapped Christmas presents with duct tape, I couldn't imagine why you wouldn't use tape. "These people are very particular and caring. Before giving this as a gift, they will untie the ribbon, open the box, and unwrap the tissue paper to be sure the candle is perfect." If the wrapping had tape, the giver couldn't do that without harming the packaging.

My mind froze. The awareness of what I just heard was greater than I could handle then and there, but it became the foundation on which

I built my business. I had stumbled upon a secret code. By not using tape when wrapping a package, Bergdorf Goodman was telling its affluent customers, "We know that you'll open this and check for flaws before you present it. We see you and we understand you." I came to call this a "secret language." It had been there all along, like a language I couldn't speak until—I could.

Realizing that I would never have known that "no tape" was so important. I knew I had plenty to learn. I knew I'd need to know it all to succeed. I had learned an inside secret. Every market has a secret language. No market or set of people was better than another. But what motivated my parents to spend their hard-earned money was very different from what inspired customers at Bergdorf Goodman. They spoke two different languages.

As I looked around, I noticed the beautiful assortment of home decorative items delicately displayed on skirted tables in separate rooms, each its own boutique. It was a far cry from the aisles of metal shelves I was used to. The entire environment and culture of the place was speaking to their ideal customer. "No tape" was part of the secret language of the affluent market.

I realized that my business wasn't failing because I wasn't good enough or because I was charging too much. My business was failing because I wasn't speaking the secret language of the market I was in nor of the market that would be best served by the business I wanted to build. I had a choice. I could employ the language of my hometown, but I didn't believe I would ever really understand not having portraits to hand down. I'd have to change myself, my beliefs, and my values. It would be easier to learn a new language. I suspect that will be the case for you too. Don't compromise who you are. Don't try to change your core values to fit in. Find the people in your current market or seek out a new one who language you can learn to speak. You can learn a "foreign" language. But it's pretty hard to learn to be a new you. Why would you want to? Be you. Allow who you are to determine whom you can best serve. Create a brand that makes it easy for them to spot you in that crowd. That's speaking their secret language.

LEARNING THE LINGO

IT'S IMPORTANT TO NOTE THAT speaking your audience's lingo is about more than brand compatibility. It's brand bonding, as the results from following the strategies laid out in this book will show you. Speaking the same lingo is making your ideal customer believe you get them and that they get you. You "get them" fully, with a deeper understanding of what they value, how they live, what inspires them to purchase, and what makes them tick with compassion and empathy.

Do you know that feeling when someone fully "gets" you? I hope you do, because there's nothing quite like it in my opinion. That person you meet with whom you instantly feel a connection and become lifelong friends in a short time. It should be the goal of every loving relationship to fully get the other person. It's an opportunity to believe someone hears us, sees us, and values who we are. Perhaps you've even picked up a book, read the description, and thought, "Wow, this author is completely speaking my language." You think you must buy this book! Effective use of the LINGO strategies will make your ideal customer believe they must work with you or interact with your brand.

In that moment in the back room of Bergdorf Goodman's gift wrap department, I realized "no tape" was part of a much bigger picture. It was one small part of a whole lingo that caused the customers of Bergdorf Goodman to know they were understood by Bergdorf Goodman. They "got" their customers. My mind all but exploded with curiosity. What else didn't I know about this culture of the affluent? What else could I learn about the power of speaking the lingo of a specific market?

What I learned that day has become the basis of every business I've built and taught to the clients I've coached. Whether the market is high-end, low-end, or anything in between, a secret language will connect your brand to the customers you want to work with. You just have to learn their lingo.

As I walked around the store, I began to notice designer labels were everywhere. Vera Wang, Diane von Furstenberg, Calvin Klein, Chanel, Christian Dior. Designer names prominently displayed created a sense of "custom" and "high-end." At the time, my photography business was not my name. I noticed there weren't any cash registers in sight. In a store where everything cost so much, there was no evidence of the exchange of money. Now, I don't know about you, but where I grew up, people going to the cash registers were lined up like cattle in pens. Consider this. Where things are less expensive, it's blatantly obvious that the store is going to take your money. Yet, in Bergdorf Goodman and many other high-end stores, the registers are discretely hidden. What's the psychology at play? For people who have money, you don't want it to be about the money. For people who don't have the money, it's more about the money. Let's get a little more abstract. Do you know that what you focus on, you get more of? People with money don't focus on spending money. They focus on the luxury, joy, and freedom that are the benefits of money. When serving the high-end market, you don't want to draw attention to the checkout process. Lower-end markets are price-conscious and focused on the careful spending of their money, which is why the registers are front and center.

Another thing I noticed as I wandered around the store was the pricing itself. First thought? "Wow, this place is expensive!" But I quickly noticed that the prices were rounded off to whole numbers. Fifty dollars. Five hundred dollars. Five thousand dollars! Not $48.02, which was the cost of my 8x10 photograph at the time! These are not nickel and dime people. Keep it simple and round it off. On the other hand, Walmart does roll-back pricing to assure their customers the lowest price imaginable—right down to the hundredth of a cent! My family used to shop in stores that would occasionally have scratch-off cards for an added discount. Everything was priced right down to the penny.

I noticed that Bergdorf Goodman had a certain look, very different from what I was accustomed to. Merchandise was displayed in a very tidy manner. There was volume, but simplicity as well. The stores I grew up going to were cluttered. Here, blue light specials were replaced with warm ambient light and spotlights accenting particular items.

I left Bergdorf Goodman fully prepared to re-brand my business and move it to where I could connect with a customer just like those who shopped at Bergdorf's. There was a lot of work to do ahead and many more visits to Bergdorf's, other high-end stores, and exclusive restaurants. But I understood clearly that to be successful, I would have to understand, speak, communicate, and think in the secret language of my ideal customers.

THE FIVE-STEP STRATEGY TO DEVELOP THE SECRET LANGUAGE OF YOUR IDEAL CUSTOMERS

ONCE I KNEW MY IDEAL customers well enough to speak their language in every aspect of my business, everything changed. Within a year I was not only serving the market I wanted to serve, I was doing five times as much business.

As soon as I knew my ideal customers secret language, being an entrepreneur did seem easy. The challenges I experienced early on disappeared or morphed into "good problems"—being overbooked, instead of overlooked. And, over time, something interesting happened. I noticed my perception of myself changed. I no longer felt like the young man collapsed on the floor in my photography studio and wondering if I'd ever succeed. I started to see myself through the eyes of my ideal customers, my people. It wasn't just that I became more confident, although that certainly happened. I started to become the person I was always meant to be. Isn't that why we got into business for ourselves anyway? Yes, we have goals and ideas. We want to make money and we want to make a difference in the world. But really, at its core, entrepreneurship is about becoming the person we were truly meant to be.

Working with our ideal customer brings out the most of whom we are capable of being. We blow people away by speaking their secret language, and that has a wonderful impact on us. What's more, they tell other people. Our businesses grow. In a few years, you have the equivalent of my eight-week waiting list.

And that process of becoming all that you're capable of being can begin with learning the secret language of your ideal customer.

Every market has a secret language—high-end, low-end, and everything in between. Armed with a far better understanding of what the world looks like from the perspective of the affluent customer, I returned home from Bergdorf Goodman prepared to build a new business speaking the secret language of the customer that I felt would most value what I had to offer.

The secret language strategy has five components. Each component has a specific intention and creates a specific result:

1. Perspective - Understand how your ideal customers experience their world.
2. Familiarity - Create an environment that feels remarkably comfortable to your ideal customers.
3. Style - Help your ideal customers make a quick decision to hire you, buy your product, and consider your business.
4. Pricing Psychology - Let your ideal customers know they're in the right place doing business with you.
5. Words - Draw in your ideal customers and filter out the rest by acting as emotional triggers.

Every market has a secret language. At its heart, the secret language strategy is about deeply knowing your ideal customer—whomever your ideal customer may be. That's the beauty of this empathetic, non-judgmental approach. It's not specifically for any particular market.

While my experience may have been about reaching the high-end, it really has nothing to do with the high-end market. It just so happens that's where I was best suited to serve. It's adaptable so that you can reach the customers that you feel you are best suited to serve, as long as you speak their language. In the next chapter, you'll define your ideal customer. You might be surprised to find out it has more to do with who you are than you might have thought.

⊛CH. 2
WHO WILL LOVE THAT?

I WANT TO CHALLENGE A well-known business theory. I'm not saying it's "wrong"; I just want to challenge its implication so that you can think differently about the results you want. I'm referring to the Pareto Principle, which is also known as the 80/20 rule. This principle states that 80 percent of your income will come from 20 percent of your customers. There are many instances where this theory is true. However, it doesn't have to be true. In fact, to believe that it does can be very detrimental to many businesses.

Can you imagine if only two out of ten customers were worth the effort? If eight out of ten didn't pay you what you were worth? That would be a nightmare! And a huge waste of your time.

What you want is a business where all, or almost all, of your customers are worth the effort and probably the easiest to do business with. It is my belief that learning and applying the secret language strategies as I have laid them out in *LINGO* will result in doing business with your ideal customer almost all the time. You no longer have to settle for only 20 percent of your customers being worth your effort.

If you were to ask me the number-one reason why my businesses are successful, my answer would be because I only work with my ideal customer. Imagine, because of a visit to Bergdorf Goodman in New

York City and developing the secret language strategies, by my late twenties I had a phenomenally successful photography business and it was simply because all my customers were exactly whom I wanted to work with. Speaking their secret language called them forward. I enjoyed working with them, there was tremendous financial reward, and they stayed my customers for decades. Aren't you ready for results like that? Don't you want every customer to be a joy to do business with? Don't you want to be irresistible to your ideal customers? Of course you do.

Working with your ideal customers requires saying yes and saying no. I know you're saying yes because you're willing to do the work to learn their secret language. Saying no is the hard part. By speaking the specific secret language of those you want to say yes to and building the brand that stands out to them above all else, you shouldn't have to say no very often.

At all times, you want customers to receive the best value from your service and benefit from your product. At all times. No exceptions. If they feel they received more value than what they paid, they will gladly pay you what you're worth. If they are thrilled with the benefits of what you offer, they will tell others. And guess what? There's a really good chance that your ideal customers are friends with people who are also your ideal customers. Ideal customers beget other ideal customers. Now you have a positive loop. A circle is forming, and a community of all ideal customers is being built.

Imagine then what happens if you break that cycle by doing business with a non-ideal customer, the customer you took on because you "needed" the business, or the one who snuck through the branding filter. The outlier customer is like a virus infiltrating your ideal customer community. You can't create exceptional value for the outlier customer. They will never be fully happy. You'll jump through hoops, do a dance, sing a song, and never satisfy the outlier customer. Meanwhile, they have sucked up valuable energy needed for your ideal customers. Could they be taking time and effort away from your ideal customers? Probably.

That could have a much greater negative impact on your business. I'm telling you, and I suspect you know it, the non-ideal, outlier customer is never worth it.

Entrepreneurs do business with the non-ideal customer because they need the money. They are in a financial pinch or think some money is better than no money. But let's think about this differently. The quickest way to comfortably say no to non-ideal customers is to not need their business. The quickest way to not need their business is to work only with your ideal customers. Otherwise, years go by when some customers are worth it, some aren't, and before you know it, only two out of ten customers are worth it.

THE BENEFITS OF ONLY WORKING WITH YOUR IDEAL CUSTOMERS

APPLYING THE SECRET LANGUAGE STRATEGIES will result in getting you ideal customers. Let's reiterate what we know about ideal customers and the benefits of building a business just for them.

- Your ideal customers are waiting for you to show up. It's your job to show up, speak their language, and make it easy for them to find you.
- Because you "get" them, you know what's going on in their heads. This makes it much easier to complete their thoughts and create self-identifying questions which you will use in marketing.
- Since they "get" you, a bond is formed.
- They want you to succeed and will be eager to talk about your business with their friends.
- Mutual commitment to creating the highest value experience enables you to be at your best at all times.
- Ideal customers are the easiest to work with.
- They already value what you have to offer, so you don't have to prove your value.

- Ideal customers tend to travel in circles of people just like them, so spreading the word about your business is easier.
- Interacting with ideal customers is joyful.
- They respect your efforts and gladly pay you what you're worth.
- It's easier to create and expand your business because you understand their needs.
- Ideal customers are loyal, lessening the pressure of having to acquire new customers.
- Because there's a similarity in buying behavior amongst your ideal customers, your business is steadier and more stable.

The key to having a successful business is doing business with your ideal customers. I stress, your ideal customers: not other businesses' customers, not the customers you'd like to have, not everyone who comes along, not the ones who challenge your prices, not the ones who make you miserable. Your ideal customer. The ones that you are for. The ones who bring you joy, are the easiest to work with, and pay you what you're worth.

I have had many coaching customers take the leap, change their businesses, and start only accepting the most ideal customers. Sometimes there's a period of panic. Often there's a dip in volume, sometimes for a while, sometimes permanently. This can be scary. You might think, "What have I done?" I've had coaching customers call me in a panic because they are not working as hard as they used to. I'll ask them, "Yes, but what do the numbers say? How do your sales compare to past years?" Most often, they realize they are making as much or more money and are working less hard, so much less hard that they were convinced business was down.

When you're not working as hard and are making the same or more money, that's a turning point. You've now created the time, space, and energy to take on more customers, which means your business grows and expands. Sales increase. More raving fans are talking about your business, which causes you to grow, perhaps to even refine your ideal customer, creating more time, space and energy for expansion. I hope you get the idea. Doing business with your ideal customers is the best, most efficient, profitable, and life-fulfilling way I know of to build the business of your dreams.

WHOM ARE YOU FOR?

WHEN YOU DEFINE YOUR IDEAL customers, you don't want to think about who you want your ideal customer to be. Instead, consider with whom you are best aligned. In marketing circles, there's a common question, "Whom are you for?" When asked that question, most people respond immediately by describing their ideal audience, the ideal target market they want to reach. I suggest you turn that question upside down and, instead of considering the audience, consider yourself first. Whom are you for? Before coming to a conclusion about your ideal customer, you must first understand yourself. And that gives rise to the paramount question: Who will love that?

Keeping in mind that the end goal is doing business with the customers you "get" and who think they "get" you as well. To accomplish that you must first know a lot about yourself.

Let's say you have a curt sense of humor. That's not for everybody! Or perhaps you tend to use vulgar language. Definitely not for everybody. I'm sure you can think of some comedians you may find funny but know they are not everyone's cup of tea. My extreme attention to detail is not for everyone, but it has served me incredibly well with affluent photography customers. Perhaps you have a very relaxed attitude about deadlines. I once worked with a vendor who was prone to take afternoons off to go surfing. While I respect the notion, it was definitely not for me and the tight ship I was trying to run to provide on-time delivery for my customers. On the other hand, an atmosphere that is too uptight and stiff will be a turnoff for some. The bottom line is, know who you are: your strengths, weaknesses, and innate personality traits. While there's always room for improvement and a standard of professionalism, we are striving not to change who you are but rather to leverage who you naturally are. Then ask, who would love that?

If a glue held you and your ideal customer together, it would be your shared values—the big, important life values. It is very difficult to try to convince someone to value something they don't already value. You'll exhaust yourself trying. In my case, I was trying to convince people that long-term thinking, having portraits to hand down from one generation to the next, is important: how children must have a record of their childhood, the value of family portraits for children to have when their parents are gone. I know all this is true—for me. But it wasn't necessarily true for the folks in my middle-class hometown. Sure, it was important to a degree. I mean, who doesn't think it's important to have photos of your family? But was it valued enough to pay top dollar? Not at all. We can say we value a lot of things. The difference is: What are the values we're willing to fight for? Willing to pay for? That's when the rubber meets the road.

If it's just not important enough to fight for and pay for, you're never going to convince someone otherwise. Since trying to convince someone to value what they don't already value is an uphill, and probably a losing, battle, and since your ideal customers are waiting for you to show up, wouldn't it be easier to just be there for them? So, you want to know what you value as it pertains to what you're offering. Why is what you're offering so important to you that you're willing to play the game day after day? What value is it fulfilling or what transformation is it creating that makes it so important to you? Because, without knowing that, you're going to give up. If you don't know what you're in it for, then don't be in it. Entrepreneurship can be challenging. You're going to need to know why you're stretching yourself day in and day out. You'll need to be clear about what life values you think are so important for others to know about and what values your success allows you to fulfill. Ask yourself, "What are my top three life values?" Once those are clear to you, once again ask yourself: "Who would love that?"

WHAT MAKES YOUR OFFERING UNIQUE?

PROBABLY THE EASIEST THING FOR you to identify is what it is that you do, create, or offer. We're always excited about what we do, which is a good thing. But we must always remember we are not for everybody. The death sentence for any business is to believe that what they offer is for everybody. "It's going to be huge, man! What I'm doing is so awesome everyone in the world is going to want it." It's great to be passionate, but no business is for everyone, and to believe it is will leave you unidentifiable to the people you could be reaching. So the next step in identifying your ideal customer is to be clear on what you do. And—you guessed it! Who would love that?

Now consider what is unique about what you offer. If your ideal customer was to write a review about your business, product, or service, what are the top three things you want every one of your ideal customers to say? This is a unique way to look at your business and helps you get very clear on what makes you unique. Sure, you can be good at many things in your business. But specifically, what are three things you want to excel at that are most important to your ideal customer?

Let's look at home renovation contractors as an example. One contractor might want to be known as the contractor who comes in on budget. He works so hard toward this goal that his customers repeatedly review his business online and point out how thrilled they were that the home renovation was completed on budget. Another home renovation contractor might excel at completing the job on time, causing her customers to give raving reviews such as how the job was done on time so their family could move in before school started. Each contractor can identify what makes their business unique. Contractor A will appeal to the cost-conscious homeowner. Contractor B will draw forward the homeowner who is more interested in timing than money. You get to decide what you want to excel at that will cause your ideal customer to leave a favorable review. Once you are clear on your unique offering, on what will garnish such raving reviews, you want to ask yourself: "Who would love that?"

The price point of your service or product is the great eliminator. You immediately eliminate large swaths of the market based on your price point. Statistically speaking, my photography customers represent half of one percent of the U.S. population. You may have heard about the top one percent of income earners? I estimate my ideal photography customers at half of that one percent. That means 99.5 percent of people are not my ideal customers. The price point that your ideal customer is accustomed to, no matter how broad or narrow, is a fit for some and not a fit for others. Whether your offer is a major expense or a bargain, you'll want to know: Who would love that?

WHAT DO YOU KNOW ABOUT YOUR IDEAL CUSTOMER?

Let's summarize. Here's what you now know about you and your offering:

- Your innate characteristics
- Your top three values
- What you do, create, or offer
- Your unique offering that would cause a positive review
- What price point you serve

The big question is: Who would love that? Now you have to answer the question with some specifics. Who are the people who would love you for who you are, share similar values, want what you offer, have a priority for your unique strength, and can afford you?

What's their age range? How do they live? What's their income range? Are they married, single, divorced, or maybe it doesn't matter? Are you better suited for men or women? What is it about who they are that would make them love you? I also want to encourage you to look for multiple audiences that would love what you're offering. It may be relatively easy to identify the first group that would love you. But keep looking. Consider other groups of people.

I had a conversation with a coach who specializes in helping women after divorce. What really stood out to me was that she described most her customers as being shocked by the divorce. She had story after story of women who hadn't seen the problems in the relationship. Perhaps the divorce was due to an affair, the distance that slowly came between them, and a lack of communication. She described her ideal customer as someone going through a divorce who feels her life "took a sudden left turn." And I truly believe this coach had the compassion and ability to help people manage the additional stress that comes along when your life has suddenly taken a left turn. I advised her to consider what other groups of people feel their life suddenly took a left turn: people who suddenly lost their job or those affected by the sudden death of a spouse, partner, or even child. The truth is, life sometimes takes a sudden left turn. That can be tragic, but it can be nice to know there's someone who can support you through these times as I believe this coach can. Imagine the increase in her coaching practice when she finds the additional groups of people who would love the compassion, the direction, and the ability to manage stress during a difficult time that she offers.

TO IDENTIFY YOUR IDEAL CUSTOMER, do the self-discovery work first. Then you can identify who would love that. That is your ideal customer. Now you can move on to The 5-Step Secret Language Strategy that will make your business irresistible.

⊛CH. 3
THE SECRET LANGUAGE OF PERSPECTIVE

As I LIFTED MY LEG over the bow, I thought, this is insane. It was clearly a rough day off the shores of Maine, and here I was climbing into a little rundown lobster boat, or "lobsta boat," as the locals called it. On the hour-long journey to the tiny island about ten miles from the coast, I often lay on my back and closed my eyes to make the bouts of nausea bearable. Eventually, the captain announced, "Okay, this is it," which was basically his command to get out of the boat.

When my friend insisted that I visit Monhegan Island, she gave no insights as to what I should expect. Still, I had ideas about what I would find: a lovely resort with plenty of amenities; delicious restaurants; charming shops featuring local art; and all the comforts of home. Because, you know, your friends know you, right? Or so I thought. What I found instead was an island of minimal accommodations, including a hotel room door that didn't lock and a bed whose missing leg had been replaced by a stack of books.

I was told, shall we say forewarned, that meals were only served during certain hours, because there was only power on the island at certain times of the day. If you missed mealtime, no food for you! And what really got my goat, not that I've ever had a goat: at the General Store, a sign over the register read, "If you can't live without The New York Times, go home." When I saw the sign I thought, maybe I should go home.

However, after I learned the only way to get back to the mainland that day was on an afternoon boat, I decided to kill a couple of hours with a walk. As I walked around, I began to take in the island's abundant natural beauty—the beautiful green moss, the rocky shoreline, the breathtaking views. In what was called the Cathedral Woods, the towering spruce and fir trees stood in elegant lines, as organized as pews in a church. And deer walked nearby. I felt a bit like Snow White. I couldn't help but look up toward the heavens. It truly was like being in a cathedral. It was magical. I was awestruck. As I made my way to the shoreline, I came upon a shipwreck—remnants of a boat that crashed in 1948. Now I was fascinated.

As I headed back toward town to catch the boat that would bring me back to the comforts and accommodations that the mainland promised, strangers would walk up and offer me a glass of wine. At first I was taken aback. But then I realized it was customary on this island to always have an extra wine glass and to offer a glass to people passing by. Then someone invited me home for dinner, where I was met by a group of twelve people. I soon discovered that many of the homes on the island are artist's residences and their owners welcome you inside to view their art. The island was full of beautiful art and some very well-known, highly acclaimed artists. I decided to give this mysterious little island one more chance and stay at least one night.

After dinner, as I was walking back to my hotel, thinking I hope the stack of books holds up, I came upon a crowd walking down the street. It seemed as if the entire island was migrating—or evacuating. Of course, I followed. Where did we end up? I'll bet you didn't guess a graveyard. Yup, a graveyard. A graveyard perched atop a hill, and it was then I realized we were there to watch the most spectacular sunset I have ever seen, even to this day. I was hooked on this enchanted little island.

I stayed on Monhegan Island for the few days I had originally planned and, when I left, regretted that I had to leave so soon.

What stood out to me after my trip was how my perspective about this place changed—relatively rapidly too. Once I let go of what I expected it to be, and was no longer burdened by comparison, judgment, or expectations, I was open to seeing things from a new perspective. What started out feeling like a huge mistake turned into one of the most memorable trips of my life. Once I saw the incredible natural beauty and the history of the island, and the creativity of the residents, I was enchanted. I began to see why people would give up certain physical comforts to stay here. When I got out of my own way, I could appreciate what this place was really about. It wasn't about the perspective that I'd brought to it. It was about what the place brought to me that I could learn from.

I've heard it said that how you look at the world is how the world looks back at you. For example, if you look at the world as an inherently unfriendly place, then, most likely, that's what you'll see in return. On the other hand, if you tend to see the world as a friendly place full of opportunities, then, by and large, you're likely to see more opportunities.

A little sidebar: I used to tell my kids as they were growing up that if you plant a weed, you're going to get a weed. You can't plant a weed and yell at it to become a flower. What we plant and how we look at the world are what we get back in return. If you ever have the chance to meet my three amazing kids, show them great respect for putting up with a father always trying to teach them philosophy. But, I digress.

This is what I love about the nature of perspective. When we open ourselves to seeing things from another perspective, we expand our worlds. We add to what's possible in our own lives. This will prove to be vitally important as the foundation to speaking the secret language of your ideal customer.

GAIN THE PERSPECTIVE OF THOSE YOU WANT TO SERVE

EARLIER IN THE BOOK, YOU read about my first visit to the exclusive, one-of-a-kind department store on Fifth Avenue in New York City— Bergdorf Goodman. Many of the LINGO strategies are predicated on this one visit to Bergdorf Goodman. The entire point of going to the store that day was so that I could understand what it was like to be a wealthy person. What did I know of what it was like to be a luxury shopper? I was a lower-middle-class kid from a small town! I knew absolutely nothing about luxury or the lifestyle of the affluent. But I did know that the ideal customer for my portrait photography business was a luxury shopper and I knew I had a lot to learn. I went to Bergdorf's to learn what the affluent market experienced when they went shopping, what kind of service they received, how the environment was set up, and yes, even how they wanted their packages wrapped. I knew there were tons I didn't know about the affluent market. So, I set out to learn everything I could because I knew it would be crucial to understand the perspective of that market.

It will be crucial for you, too, to learn everything you can about the perspective of your customers. It's fair to say that if, for the most part, we are not in exactly in the same place as those we serve, we likely don't fully know their perspective. It may be that we were once where they are, but we aren't now. Or we may have once known their struggle but we are past it now. As examples: Let's say you're an app developer. You may have recognized a need for this app because it solves a problem you had. Now that you've created the solution, you are no longer in the need stage; you are in the solving stage. Now, your perspective has changed. Or, perhaps you're a life coach. You are likely handing out your wisdom and helping people who are at least a couple of steps behind you in their personal development. Can you still tap into the perspective you had when you were experiencing similar challenges?

Your ideal customer may be someone who is better off than you are right now. Or, they may have a cultural background you don't share. Perhaps they're in a different age group. They may have goals that are different from yours or have experienced problems you never experienced. Your ideal customers may come from a part of the world you've never visited.

Understanding this is important, because it means you have some learning to do about the perspective of those you want to serve. Gaining their perspective, like my visit to a tiny island, will probably take more than an afternoon. Metaphorically speaking, to see the world through their eyes, you'll have to take a walk around a bit, meet some locals, and enjoy their customs.

Here's a little tip: I have my coaching clients journal their experiences as we work together. They do this because their growth is going to be rapid and they will want to remember what it was like to be where the people they serve are. Later, it helps them regain an understanding of their ideal customer's perspective. So track your progress as you grow.

WALK A MILE IN THEIR SHOES

YOU'VE PROBABLY HEARD THE PHRASE "you don't truly understand someone until you've walked a mile in their shoes." It's really true, and the statement is intended to encourage empathy and compassion. When we understand where someone is coming from—their perspective—we are more likely to empathize with them and offer compassion. That's the premise of the TV show *Undercover Boss*. Bosses, CEOs, and high-level managers take on an alias, don a disguise, and interact with employees in their own businesses. It's an eye-opening experience for the undercover boss, and the outcome of every episode is nearly always the same: both the boss and the employees have a better understanding of one another because they now can see from one another's perspective.

Walking a mile in your ideal customer's shoes is the best way for you to understand their perspective. If you can go to the places where your ideal customers hang out, please go! Visit the retail establishments, the restaurants, the parks, the museums, the ballfields, and the stadiums. If you can, go undercover.

Speaking of undercover, the first time I went to Bergdorf Goodman, I was wearing a Members Only jacket, cargo pants—blue cargo pants—with shoes that had holes in them. I'd like to think my sense of style has improved considerably. Follow me on social media and let me know.

In any case, if you have the opportunity to visit physical locations that are similar to where your ideal customers would go, do. Take in all the details. What does the physical environment look like? What are the common colors, scents, and sounds? Is it loud or quiet? Are there long lines or do people sit and wait to be served? Is the staff wearing uniforms? Notice how the customers and salespeople behave and interact. What expectations are being met? What does it feel like?

As you research your ideal customer's perspective, pay attention to the lingo people use. At one time during my own research, I was visiting five-star hotels in New York City because I figured my ideal customers stayed at similar hotels when they traveled. While at one of the hotels I had a realization. I thought, if my ideal customers are staying here, how can I meet them?

It dawned on me that I could ask the concierge for help. But how could I get an in with the concierge? Talk about needing to know the lingo! The world of concierges has a lingo of its own. Do you know what the person in charge of all the concierges is called? I didn't. Head concierge? Nope. The person in charge is called Chef Concierge. Who would have thought? In French, the word Chef means Chief. So, really, you are referring to the Chief Concierge, which makes sense, right? But who would have thought Chef Concierge? I'm glad I did my homework.

You might be wondering why I thought to ask. Well, any time you are heading toward something unfamiliar, be curious as to whether there is a secret language—every time. Treat your research expedition as if you are going to a foreign country and you need to learn enough of the language to fit in with the locals—or at least find your way around.

Matters of etiquette are a form of lingo as well. Raising my kids, I made my best attempt to teach them the lingo of etiquette—what utensils to use, what behaviors are considered to be good manners, and so on. For instance, I taught my adult children that, at a cocktail party, always hold your drink in your left hand so your right hand, the one you shake with, isn't cold or wet from your drink. When my son attended one of his first political events in Washington, D.C., he called me from the restroom asking me for a crash refresher course on the lingo of etiquette. One of those satisfying moments as a parent happens when you knew they would regret tuning you out. Speaking of politics, there certainly is a lingo. A President, present or past, is always referred to as Mr. (or someday Madame) President. There are lots of rules of lingo around politics, heads of state, and important gatherings.

What if you're not fortunate enough to physically visit places that your ideal customer goes to? Consider how else you can do this research. How else can you live in their world so that you can gain their perspective? Maybe it's by reading the magazines or blogs that they read. Perhaps you'll gain a better understanding of their perspective by paying attention to their lifestyles. What charities do they support, if any? What social events do they attend? What holidays do they observe? Are there common experiences your ideal customers share? For example, do they all migrate to the lake every summer? Or are they all Black Friday ninja shoppers, poised and ready with their coupon circulars outside the stores just hours after the Thanksgiving leftovers are packed away? You have the advantage of online research that didn't exist when I was starting out. You can accomplish a tremendous amount online to understand the lifestyle, preferences, likes, and dislikes of your ideal customer.

Are there common behaviors amongst those you serve? Can you describe them a certain way? Introverted? Outgoing? Are they typically optimistic and success-minded? Or are they pessimistic and thinking everyone is out to get them?

Or can you imagine what their top values are? My coaching clients, for example are, across the board, seekers. It doesn't matter what their lifestyles are, how diverse their industries; they are constantly seeking to grow personally and professionally. What does this tell me about their perspective? They believe the world is full of opportunities—and frustrations. That's because, inherently, when you see the world as full of opportunities, you get frustrated when you don't achieve everything you set out to achieve as quickly as you'd like. Knowing this about my ideal customers, I can understand their emotional perspective.

No matter how diverse your customers may be, look for what is in common in the way they live, their career paths, how they behave, and what they value.

My designer coaching client, Lancia, was setting out to serve a super-high-end clientele with her custom-made invitations and corporate gift boxes. To understand the perspective of her ideal customer, what we referred to as people living a very "polished" lifestyle, I asked her to research the highest-end products she could find online. She found chartered jets and extraordinarily expensive bottles of champagne, exclusive fragrances, and luxury resorts. Doing this type of research accomplishes several things. For one, it opens your mind to things you probably never knew about. Did you know there's such a thing as a three thousand-dollar bottle of champagne? Or even nearly twelve thousand? Just Google "most expensive bottles of champagne." This is normal for some people. It may not be normal from your perspective. But from someone else's, it is. My client was able to use the information she gathered to better position her own offering. She began to know the secret language of the customers she wanted to attract. She also gained some good marketing words she could use!

YOUR RESEARCH HAS COMPOUND VALUE

ALWAYS QUESTION WHETHER THERE IS a lingo to learn anytime you venture into unchartered territory. At the five-star Manhattan hotels, I suspected there might be a lingo in the concierge industry. Sure enough, there was. How did I figure it out? I first turned to Google for the answer. Then, I confirmed the information was right by asking the concierge at the first hotel I went to. Having discovered this, I was able to ask for the Chef Concierge at many five-star hotels in New York City, where I lived at the time. The Chef Concierge, who managed the main database the other concierges referred to when there was a request from a guest, would be the one to spread the word to the rest of the staff. I introduced myself and my portrait photography services and gained their referrals to families visiting from around the world. Often, guests would think of a family portrait once they arrived in the city. In other cases, the concierge would suggest the idea.

Because I discovered the appropriate lingo for five-star hotels, I now know that, when visiting these hotels, nothing would have been sloppier than not asking for the person in charge by the correct title. I'm sure the fact I knew they were called Chef Concierge put me in the inner circle. I was speaking their lingo, so they would introduce me to my ideal customers. In this way, my research had a compound benefit: I learned more about my affluent customer base and I gained customers through referrals.

NONJUDGMENT IS VITAL TO UNDERSTANDING YOUR IDEAL CUSTOMER'S PERSPECTIVE

As I QUICKLY LEARNED ON my trip to Monhegan Island, it is important that you have no preconceived judgements or assumptions about your ideal customers. Wipe the slate clean of what you think you know, if anything, and be open to understanding the other's perspective first.

I'll be honest; growing up, I heard a lot of assumptions about "rich people." You know, "Their kids are raised by nannies." "They have money but they're actually miserable." "Money is the root of all evil." I'm glad I didn't buy into any of that because, in my research and subsequent interactions with affluent customers, I didn't find any of those stereotypes to be true, not one. I found quite the opposite. I discovered that financial freedom gives people the opportunity to choose what they prioritize, which, in most cases, is family. And I learned that, while money may not buy happiness, it sure does afford the opportunity to go to places where fun and happiness can be found!

To truly understand someone else's perspective, let go of your preconceived ideas. This is not to say you have to agree with everyone's point of view. By all means, if someone's values conflict with your own values, you have every right to not work with that person. But it is important to be open and understanding of this new perspective that you're getting a chance to explore. Isn't not understanding someone else's perspective the root of most arguments? You want to find the clients with whom you have no conflict, whose perspective you understand and respect. You may not aspire to live like them, and that's fine. But if you want to serve them, you must understand, empathize with, and respect them.

◆

WITH YOUR NEWFOUND PERSPECTIVE, YOU'LL be able to build on everything you'll learn in the remaining steps of The Secret Language Strategy. You will have the information and understanding you'll need to build a business for exactly the customers you want to work with. You'll know what the world looks like from their perspective in the literal sense and you'll have a deeper understanding of what they value. You may not be like them or desire to be like them. And that's fine. But if you want to serve them and gain their trust and their business, you certainly better understand their perspective. In fact, in my opinion, you're not entitled to your ideal customers' business unless you've walked a mile in their shoes.

⊙CH. 4
THE SECRET LANGUAGE OF FAMILIARITY

WHO WOULD HAVE THOUGHT YOU could create an uproar over a biscuit? Apparently, I can. As is true for most American families, my family has strict traditions when it comes to Thanksgiving. We gather at my mother's house for dinner with turkey, stuffing, cranberry sauce, and biscuits. For as long as I can remember, the biscuit of choice was the kind that came in a cardboard tube you would smack on the edge of the counter until it exploded to reveal the white, doughy biscuits. As kids, we would argue over who got the privilege of taking tube to counter.

One year, well into my thirties with kids of my own, I suggested to my mother, "Why don't I make biscuits from scratch this year?" I enjoy baking and I was also trying to bring a touch of sophistication to my family.

Mom agreed, and I spent days planning: choosing the best recipe; making the dough; cutting the biscuits; baking them just in time so they were slightly crispy on the outside, soft and steamy on the inside as you split them open. I truly thought I had created the perfect biscuits and raised the standard of fine dining for my family.

Everything went perfectly... until my family sat down to dinner.

There was an uproar! Everyone had a fit that I had broken a tradition. My younger cousins felt robbed of their opportunity to break open the tube of biscuits. There was criticism that my biscuits, while tasty, were heavier than the "normal" biscuits. It was a complete smackdown. Not only were they not impressed, they were angry. I realized then you just don't mess with tradition.

Traditions are important to your customers. If you offer them the equivalent of scratch biscuits when they expect and want biscuits in a can, you might get your own smack-down. In 2010, the Gap attempted to change their logo after twenty years: not their name or even their familiar logo colors, just the font and design of the logo. Instead of Gap in a serif font within a blue box, it was changed to a san serif font with a small blue box intersecting the "p" in Gap. Their loyal customer base went nuts! Criticism spread like a wildfire on social media. Despite the Gap's official statement that they appreciated the "passionate debates," they retracted and went back to the traditional logo within a week. That's how passionate and attached customers can become to what is familiar to them.

Now, if your brand is not familiar to your prospective customers, you won't get a smackdown. You won't hear anything at all, because your ideal customers will just keep on walking. They'll do this because they don't feel a connection with you.

What's familiar to us creates an instant connection. I experienced this on a flight to New York City. It was one of those extremely rare times when I was stuck in the middle seat. As I sat down, I noticed the fortunate guy who would be next to me in the window seat was reading a book by an author who had been booked to be a guest on a Creative Warriors podcast just two days earlier. It was a pretty big deal that we landed this guest. Although I had never read any of his books, he's known to be highly respected for his work and has a considerable audience. It's always helpful when a guest has significant influence to spread the word about the podcast.

THE SECRET LANGUAGE OF FAMILIARITY 47

Since my rowmate was reading this book by this well-known author and since I knew nothing about the book, I struck up a conversation. I mentioned that we had just booked the author as a podcast guest.

Jason, as his name turned out to be, told me he also has a podcast. In fact, we were leaving the same convention. With so much in common, we had a nice, long conversation on the way home, have become good friends since, and I consider Jason to be a trusted business associate, an all-around great guy.

What struck me most is, that had he not been reading that book, I would not have struck up a conversation. I fly a lot. I'm friendly with my neighboring passengers, but usually more than happy to keep to myself to get work done or sleep (usually sleep). I spoke up only because he was reading a book that I had a connection to. I spoke up when I typically would not have. Had he been reading *Ten Masochistic Things to Do on a Friday Night*, I probably would not have spoken up because, for better or for worse, that's not familiar to me.

That's the power of familiarity. What's familiar to us creates an instant connection. How many times have you heard about something for the first time and then suddenly it seems like it's everywhere? Have you ever traveled abroad? What happens when you see brands familiar from your homeland? How do you feel? Typically, those familiar brands stand out from everything else. Usually you will have a feeling of comfort. Why do comfort food and traditions make us feel all warm and fuzzy inside? Because they are familiar. Macaroni and cheese or turkey with stuffing and gravy remind us of our childhood and family gatherings. Comfort food makes us feel, well, comfortable.

The basis of any language is familiarity. When I moved from New York City to a predominantly Spanish-speaking community in Miami Beach, I realized everyone else's dogs understood Spanish. Of course, a dog is going to respond to whatever language they're trained with.

It just never occurred to me until I witnessed it firsthand. So, really, there's no basis for language, how we speak it and how we hear it, other than the fact that we are trained in sounds that are familiar which create a language. We become fluent in what is familiar. That's our comfort zone.

Even technology has caught on to the benefits of familiarity. That's how the algorithms work when you shop online on sites like Amazon and there are suggestions for you phrased as "customers also bought." It's also the basis behind tracking pixels, which track web pages you visit and cause those products to magically appear on your Facebook wall. All these technologies get the power of familiarity. It is very likely that if you enjoy a particular book or purchase a certain product, there's a good chance that you'll be interested in other products that are similar. Or if you didn't purchase the first time, if it repeatedly shows up on Facebook, you might purchase at another time. Even as an advertiser on Facebook, you can create what are called "look-alike audiences." You can target one group based on the behavior of another group. Basically you're assuming that if something is familiar to group A, there's a good chance group B, being a similar group, will also be interested. It will be familiar to them as well. As technology and the advancement of algorithms continues to get more and more human, it's interesting to see how they rely on the human emotion of familiarity for purchasing decisions. So why wouldn't you?

Again, what is familiar to us makes us feel comfortable and creates an instant connection. When your brand—your office, your storefront, your business card, your voicemail message, your website—seems familiar to your ideal customers, it is much easier for you to attract them, and keep them. You've made sure your brand will feel familiar because you understand their perspective. When they feel that sense of familiarity—when they recognize you—not only do they feel comfortable with you, they feel certain about you. What could be more magnetic than that?

ATTRACT YOUR IDEAL CUSTOMERS AND FILTER OUT THE REST

THE MOST IMPORTANT REASON FAMILIARITY is an essential part of speaking your audience's secret language is that familiarity will attract your ideal customers and filter out the rest. Think about it. Since we are drawn to what is familiar and comfortable to us, we, as the buyers, are going to self-identify whether or not we want to connect with your brand. Think of it as the "familiarity filter."

For example, Old Country Buffet restaurant was familiar to my family. I'll bet most rich people know nothing about Old Country Buffet. Jo Malone fragrances for the bathroom mean nothing to my family. Yet they are in the bathroom of almost every wealthy person's home—at least those I've been in. Familiarity indicates lifestyle just like brands indicate lifestyle. The brands we buy say something about how we live and what we can afford.

Many people shop at Whole Foods for their meat and produce, yet stop by Costco for their paper goods. But even still, you can define where your business fits into the market. Why would someone shop at Whole Foods for meat and produce and Costco for paper goods? It's much more of a hassle to go to both places. It's because, when it comes to nourishing their family, they may feel that paying the extra price at Whole Foods (lovingly referred to as whole paycheck) is worth every dime. Being far less emotionally attached to paper goods, that same consumer may go to Costco.

What does this tell you about positioning your business? If your business is a luxury item, then you're going to want to speak the language of personal fulfillment: how your product or service will enrich their lives, where "you get what you pay for" evokes a desire to have the best. Or, in Whole Foods case, the healthiest. However, if your brand is practical, a necessity, more of a commodity, then people are likely to be more price-conscious. What's different in today's world is buyers will cross market segments—high-end for what enriches their life, lower-end for necessities. Speak the proper language of the market segment you are aiming for.

This is the crazy, yet very important thing to understand about secret languages: They are already there, right under your nose, and you don't know it. You don't know it because, if it's not the language you speak, you don't hear it or you don't understand it.

As a lifelong entrepreneur, I hear corporate people talking in acronyms, and about 360s, and all sorts of things I have no idea about. Just a few years ago, I had to ask someone what C-Suite meant. For years I heard people refer to C-Suite, but I was too embarrassed to ask. It clearly meant something to other people, but to me, it was literally a foreign language. Once I asked, I learned C-Suite refers to the offices of all the executives with a "C" in their title—CEO, CFO, COO, and so on.

The world of business is divided into many different market segments, often by price point, but also by things such as behavior patterns, age, gender, and various demographics. Think of these market segments as wave lengths. Like channels on the radio, multiple signals are being sent, all at the same time. While you're listening to the music you like, say pop, you're aware there are other channels that you're not listening to: country, jazz, rap. Different channels, different signals for different audiences, are all being broadcast at the same time, yet you just listen to what you want to hear. Secret languages are similar. They're already there. Brands, market segments, and audiences are already aligned and listening to one another. Familiarity determines the channel that you choose to tune into.

What channel do you want to be on, and who do you want your "listener" to be? Familiarity sends the signal. Once we understand what is familiar to the ideal customer we are trying to attract, we can create situations that are attractive and magnetic to that specific ideal customer.

Familiarity is efficient. That's not to say you shouldn't be creative and innovative. But when it comes to positioning and attracting the right customers, don't reinvent the wheel. They've already carved out a market segment, a signal they are tuned into. Just jump on board. Creating from what's already familiar to your ideal customer is the fastest way I know to get the results you want.

HOW DO I USE FAMILIARITY?

THIS IS WHERE KNOWING THEIR perspective and "walking in their shoes" is going to really pay off. In order to discover what is familiar to your ideal customer and attract them by creating that familiarity, you must have walked in their shoes.

So let's start with what you can do to find out what is familiar to your ideal customer if you are in a similar geographical location. If you can, go to the brick and mortar locations of the stores and brands your ideal customers currently buy from. Go to the restaurants, places of entertainment, hangouts, and services they use and study the hell out of these places!

1. How would you describe the atmosphere? Is it warm and friendly or bright and fast-moving?
2. Are the brands they are drawn to high-volume chains or custom-oriented?
3. What's the price point? Are they frequenting high-end brands, low-end, or somewhere in between? Are the prices visible or hidden?
4. What kind of music is playing, if any?
5. Is there enough staff to give individual assistance, or are the customers pretty much on their own?
6. Observe the brands they purchase, the businesses they visit, and the products they buy. Based on this information, what do you think are their top three values? Do they value quality, saving time, saving money, personal fulfilment, making money, having an impact, fame, tradition, convenience, or what among so many others?

Take Target department store for example. What do you think is the top value for people who shop at Target? It's not price. It's value. Target is all about getting top-name designers for less money. For years, Target has featured couture designers such as Isaac Mizrahi, Lilly Pulitzer, and Vera Wang, giving access to high-end designers that we ordinary folks wouldn't normally be able to afford. Of course, the clothes offered at Target are not couture outfits. But shoppers at Target believe they are getting more value for the price because of the draw of these big name designers. Target makes chic affordable. So one of the values of the typical Target shopper is "value"—believing you're getting more than you paid for.

I mentioned Whole Foods. Whole Foods shoppers value nourishment, healthy living, the impact on the environment, providing the best for their family, and good taste. You could say the Whole Food shopper believes in a bigger picture for a healthy world and sustainable planet. For some people, shopping at Whole Foods feels like being part of a movement, and they are willing to pay more for that.

What if your ideal customer frequents Ikea? What do you think they value? It certainly isn't saving time! Saving time being one of my top life values, Ikea drives me nuts! You're stuck on this line and have to meander through the store in the manner they want you to. You can occasionally take a shortcut, but for the most part you are like cattle being herded. No quickly running in at Ikea. Then you have to go to the warehouse and pick out your own merchandise. Who thought of something so sadistic? And putting together the items? Do we even have to discuss this? There is definitely no saving time at Ikea.

Don't get me wrong. I admire Ikea as a brand and how they've called forward their ideal customer using secret language techniques. But they certainly are not speaking the language of saving time. So what do Ikea customers value? For one, price. The deals can be amazing. I'd say value as well. You can get (after you have painstakingly put together) furniture that looks far more expensive than it cost. Ikea shoppers value experience. Let's face it, it's just a Mickey Mouse or two away from Disney World. But one of the most driving life values of the Ikea shopper is personal fulfillment. If you've survived the Ikea shopping experience, you've accomplished something. When you go home and put together that crib for your child, wall unit for your living room, or desk for your new office, you have reached true heights of personal fulfillment. Ikea shoppers are do-it-yourselfers and darn proud of it!

Visiting the establishments of brands that your ideal customer is already doing business with will help you understand the experience and see life from their perspective. This doesn't mean you have to visit the exact same location or even the exact same brand. Brands that are reaching the same audience will work. But what if you can't? What do you do if you are nowhere near brands or the lifestyle of your ideal customer? Fortunately, you always have the Internet. My suggestion is to read blogs or lifestyle magazines that pertain to your ideal customer. The key is understanding their lifestyle and behaviors.

When I was just starting out to serve affluent customers, magazines like Town & Country became my resource for learning about their lifestyle. The articles and content on blogs will show you what's important to your ideal customers, and what they're interested in reading about. The graphic design and photos will showcase the styles and looks that are familiar to them. The advertisers will inform you of brands that are trying to reach the same audience. Again, it's a version of walking in their shoes. Read the publications they're reading. Go to the blogs they're visiting.

As you set out to understand the brands, businesses, and products your ideal customer already interacts with, keep in mind that they may be interacting with brands you don't know at all because they are listening to a "different channel." If you listened to a radio station of a genre of music you never listen to, there would be ads for products that are not at all familiar. Once you might have brushed something off as not being very popular because you never heard of it; now it's great to learn about brands you never knew existed. You are honing in and getting to know your ideal customer at a whole new level.

CREATE FAMILIAR ENVIRONMENTS

NOW YOU'RE READY TO APPLY what you have learned, to use what is familiar to your ideal customer. I call this "creating environments." The establishments you visited and the magazines and blogs you read all created an environment, a feeling. You want to create a similar feeling wherever your ideal customer will interact with your brand. Make them feel like they belong there. They should feel the comfort of familiarity.

Start right at the beginning, when customers first interact with your brand. Is that your website? While you want your website to be unique, in what ways can it also seem similar to other brands they frequent? That doesn't mean just capturing a similar feeling as the websites of those brands. It's also what you can learn from the physical location, social media, and other promotional materials used by those brands.

Now is a good time to revisit your top three values which you identified in Chapter 2. Your website, storefront, or dog-grooming mobile must be familiar to your ideal customers, but it also must be true to your core values. The key is figuring out how to create an environment that is familiar to your people and authentic to you.

Of course, an effective brand is consistent across all fronts. I'm a huge fan of the idea of cross-industry innovation. You can learn from other industries and businesses that are completely different than your own. Cross-industry innovation offers you an opportunity to take a very fresh look at your business, give it a twist, and end up standing out from others in your industries.

One of my favorite guests on Creative Warriors is Julie Cottineau, author of *Twist: How Fresh Perspectives Build Breakthrough Brands*. She explains how the idea came to her to "mash up" brands in order to force a different perspective. She was in an airport, waiting at the gate. As she looked outside at the planes on the tarmac, much to her shock, one of the planes had the classic McDonald's golden arches on the side of the plane. She thought, "really, McDonald's has gone into the airline business?" She then realized it was a reflection of the McDonald's golden arches behind her at the gate that perfectly "landed" on the plane. It didn't take her long to realize this was an illusion. More importantly though, it got her thinking, "what would it look like if McDonald's went into the airline business?" This observation led her to the idea of mashing up brands, giving them a twist, in order to take a fresh look, to have a new perspective.

That's the point I'm stressing here: You don't have to copy what other brands have done or take ideas from their websites to apply to your website. Instead, "mash up" what you've learned about these other brands from all their assets, online and offline, and apply those ideas to your website. Are the brands your customers like contemporary or traditional? How do familiar brands present their merchandise in the store as well as online? Is the presentation cluttered or simple? Do you get a sense of the price point of these familiar brands? Are they accessible for everybody, exclusive, or right for a particular market? Is their focus on a particular age bracket or gender? What about colors and tones? Are they drawn to vibrant tones or subtler, earthy tones? All of these things are style elements which you'll read more about in the next chapter.

In the end, your website may not look anything like any other brand, but it will feel familiar to your ideal customers. It will be in the same genre, similar to when Amazon suggests a book. It's not the same book or even the same author. But if you bought one book in the self-help genre, there's a good chance you might be interested in other titles in the self-help genre.

What's the next interaction customers have with your brand? Perhaps an inquiry, be it a contact form, email, or even placing an order. Again, is the process and response what they expect from brands they like? I've seen many breakdowns in the secret language here. The experience up to this point can seem so personal and genuine, and then all of a sudden the ordering process or order confirmation is a complete departure. What was a very personal process now feels automated and generic.

In the world of online marketing it's so important that what is familiar also be consistent. If you look at the statistics, it's amazing to see how people can fall off as they go through your online process. Let's say someone sees your Facebook ad. Great. They click on the link. Cool. There's an option for something for free. Awesome. Now they need to enter an email in order to get your free thing. At any step in this process, if there's a break in consistency of branding and familiarity, I can tell you for certain they will drop off. People want to think they are walking down the same consistent, familiar path they started on. If there are any "sharp turns" or breaks in communication, they are out of there.

If you serve your ideal customers at a physical location, then of course you want it to feel homelike and familiar to them. Every interaction you have with your customers is an opportunity to create an environment, be it virtual or literal. Use the power of familiarity to trigger the feelings of comfort and belonging and you will have singled out your ideal customers and made them feel right at home.

WHAT IF YOUR IDEAL CUSTOMERS ARE DIVERSE?

SOMETIMES, YOUR IDEAL CUSTOMERS COME from different walks of life. Some might be high-end, others low-end. They may have different levels of success, be geographically diverse, even have different goals and objectives. What do you do? Let's say you're a graphic designer. You might be called upon to create a huge range of designs by a broad range of people—everything from a logo to laying out the pages of an entire book. While you might specialize in one or two services, most creatives enjoy the opportunities to do many different things. The people coming to you for your services might be from all walks of life—corporate, personal, rural, urban, high-end, and low-end. First you want to consider whether you have a specialty area.

Is there an area of expertise within graphic design that you want to be known for? Say, you specialize in graphic design for sports-oriented businesses. As a business coach, the first thing I would ask is, "if you're going to own that space, be known for sports oriented graphic designs, is there enough of a market for that?" I suspect there is. It doesn't mean that's the only thing you'll do, but it becomes your "space" when you and your business become synonymous with sports-oriented designs.

Once you are clear on the space you'll own, imagine the wide range of customers who have a need for your area of expertise. Yes, they will likely be very diverse. But I'll bet there are common characteristics amongst that diverse group. They may live wildly different lives, but I'll bet they share some aspects of the way they look at the world and have some life values in common.

For example, if you're a business having anything to do with sports, you may see the world in a competitive way, maybe not always having to be the best (although that might be true), but having to try your best, to give it your all. You are likely action oriented. The Nike "Just Do It" slogan may resonate with you. Those attitudes, life values, and worldviews may be shared by ideal customers from various walks of life. Understanding these things is your entrée into understanding who they are, what makes them tick, and what is familiar to them.

◆

CREATING A SENSE OF FAMILIARITY will give your ideal customer the comfort of knowing they are in the right place, and your business will stand out above the noise. With an understanding of your ideal customer's perspective, you can now create environments and experiences that are familiar to them, whether brick and mortar or a website.

⊛CH. 5
THE SECRET LANGUAGE OF STYLE

ACCORDING TO RESEARCH DONE BY Microsoft, a goldfish has an attention span of nine seconds. The average human has an attention span of eight seconds. Yes, a goldfish has a longer attention span than we do. And over the years, our ability to stay focused has decreased! Researchers found that since the year 2000, coincidentally around the time when the mobile revolution began, the average attention span has dropped from twelve seconds to eight seconds.

Now, I'm not a researcher, but in defense of mobile technology (and because I'm obsessed with my mobile devices), I can imagine the speed at which we live today is also a factor. We zip by things, hopping from one thing to another in an effort to get through our days. Whatever the reason, as business owners we have to acknowledge the impact this fast pace has on our businesses. Potential customers are zipping by us. They rush past our storefronts, scroll past our ads, and race through our websites. If the research is correct, we have about eight seconds to hold someone's attention, which means we probably have much less time to catch their attention.

Think about the last time you booked travel online. You glance at your options as you scroll through search engine results, online retailers, and travel booking sites. Sometimes you click, sometimes you don't. What is this quick decision based on? Or consider shopping at a store like TJ Maxx where clothing is grouped by size, not by designer. We flip through the shirts quickly, sliding the hangars as we go. Why do we stop at one particular shirt? We pay attention when style resonates with us. Knowing the style of the secret language of your ideal customer helps them make a quick decision to choose you.

As you learned in the previous chapter, the secret language of familiarity is about how things feel. You are going for the feeling of comfort that comes along with what is familiar. The secret language of style is different—it's about how things look. I'm not talking about the shallow aspects of style. (I live in Miami Beach. I know a thing or two about the shallowness of life when it's only about appearances.) No. What we're talking about here is style as a decision-maker. Speaking the secret language of style is creating recognition, having your ideal customers qualify themselves because your style resonates for them, and helping them make a quick decision.

How would you feel if I made you dress in a style that is completely out of your comfort zone? Would you like squeezing into skinny-leg jeans from Abercrombie & Fitch if you're normally a Wrangler jeans guy? Or would you love the glitz and sequins of Juicy Couture if you're a classic Talbots kind of gal? Hillary Clinton has always been made fun of for her pantsuits. But can you imagine what it would look like if she showed up in a wide-collared lacy peasant dress? Oh good lord, no! Whatever style you choose is like choosing a lane. Sure we switch lanes now and then, maybe even run off the road a few times, but we don't go down freeways in the wrong direction. When we choose a style in life that we like, be it contemporary, traditional, eclectic, urban, chic, flowery, or any other of the millions styles one can choose, really we're choosing a lane. There are things we like and things we don't. Style is a lane. When you are speaking the secret language of style of your ideal customer, you are showing up in their lane. And they recognize you for it.

My friend Tamsen Webster is a devotee of the Diane von Furstenberg® brand. Seriously—I'm not sure I've ever seen her wearing anything but a DVF dress. A keynote speaker and presentation strategist, Tamsen spends a lot of time on the stage—either physically, or when networking, or creating training videos, or conducting one of her Red Thread messaging workshops. Her love of the DVF brand is rooted in her own style and the style she wants to convey to audiences and prospective clients.

I interviewed Tamsen about her devotion to DVF, and she explained, "When I wear Diane von Furstenberg designs, the brand speaks on my behalf. The brand is timeless, sophisticated, intellectual, playful, thoughtful, and current. These are the same descriptors I want applied to my work and how I'm seen."

We can usually tell almost right away whether a brand fits us. I travel a considerable amount and am always booking hotels. I will look for certain brands of hotel pretty consistently because I like their style. I prefer hotels on the contemporary side. It's always nice to have a few brands you can rely on. However, if I'm perusing websites looking for a hotel, I decide if I'm going to look further into a hotel entirely based on the photos and style. It has to be clean, modern, and interesting to get my attention. Every now and then I can enjoy a hotel that's over-the-top grand and traditional, but by and large, the contemporary hotels get my attention. How about you? Can you think of instances where you're perusing or scrolling and something gets your attention? What is it that grabs you? What gets your attention and motivates you to stop to get more details?

You can imagine then the value of creating a style for your business that really "speaks" to your ideal customer—a style that stops them in their tracks, fits into their personality, and inspires them to take action by choosing you. In this chapter, we'll talk about the style of everything your ideal audience sees: your website, your storefront, your promotional materials, logo, packaging, and so on. Later, we'll address style in terms of pricing and the words we use to communicate with customers.

DOES YOUR STYLE FIT YOUR IDEAL CUSTOMER?

WHEN I FIRST STARTED MY photography business in the high-end market, almost immediately there was a demand for me to create photo holiday greeting cards. You know, the ones with photos mounted on the front. This was way before digitally printed cards and, believe it or not, before photo-mounted cards were readily available. I got request after request to provide holiday greeting cards with the family photo or portrait of the children on the front. Since no preprinted cards that would incorporate a photo-mount were readily available, I decided to create my own. I came up with the concepts, hired an artist to draw the artwork, and had a printer hand silkscreen the designs.

This was my first entry into understanding the secret language of style. Cards my customers would be happy to send out had to not only speak their language but also "speak" to the recipients of the cards. In other words, the cards had to speak their style—just as Tamsen's Diane von Furstenberg clothing speaks to her style.

To get to know their style, I looked at their lifestyle. I took inspiration from their landscaped homes and glanced through lifestyle magazine to get ideas from other companies and products. Picking up on design elements of their lifestyle and adding it to a card design was like sending cues that "I know how you live." For example, the community has a fair number of horse farms and a polo club, sort of a "country gentleman" style. So we added French horns to the card designs to fit into that country gentleman, equestrian lifestyle. I noticed that when their homes were decorated for the holidays, the stair banisters and fireplace mantles were decorated with boxwood greenery instead of the pine roping I grew up with. In case you're not familiar with it, boxwood is a small leaf plant that is easily shaped and is perfect to edge driveways and flower beds. During the holidays, boxwood branches are tied together to adorn mantles and bannisters. We created card designs with boxwood borders.

The cards were a sensation. In fact, it's fair to say that having customers mail tens of thousands of greeting cards with my photos on the front may have been why my reputation grew so quickly and why I was successful. The card designs, so carefully speaking their secret language of style, also let the community at large know that this guy, this young photographer, really gets our lifestyle. And it all happened because I took it upon myself to learn the style of my ideal customers and created designs that fit their taste. The right style for the right customer is a marriage made in heaven.

So seek to discover the style of your ideal customer. Look at all the aspects of their lives for information and inspiration. Just because I was designing holiday cards doesn't mean I looked at other holiday cards. Not at all! In fact, that's the last thing I would want to do. That would be assuming someone else or some other company understood my ideal customers' secret language better than I did. Trust your ability to get inside the minds and lifestyle of your ideal customers. Appreciate the desire and generosity you have in order to be willing to understand your ideal customers this intimately.

Consider the classic Ralph Lauren Polo logo. Very recognizable, speaks to a certain lifestyle, and created the preppy trend. This look that Ralph Lauren captured was very intentional and targeted to the lifestyle of his ideal customers. You even have an idea of the price point. It's a polo pony, for goodness sake. Obviously it's not going to be cheap!

All the visual elements of style create a fit for your ideal customers. You want them to feel as though the style of your brand fits them and they, in turn, are a fit for your business. That's what enables someone to make a quick decision, because they can tell right away that you are a fit for their style.

Have you ever paid attention to the thoughts running through your mind as you walk down a main shopping street or a mall? Try it next time. Pay attention to the thoughts and decisions going on in your head. Your stroll past the stores and brands on display will probably go something like this: You'll look to the left and think, "Nope, not for me." You'll look to the right, "Nope, not for me." Maybe you'll glance ahead and think, "Now that looks interesting." All this conversation in your head is based on what? Style. It's the image portrayed to get your attention. The logo design, font choice, the signage, the window displays, the marketing words, the style of the products—everything visually and collectively provides an instant feeling as to what you can expect when you step in. The style of every store and brand is right for you or it's not.

Major retail chains rarely get this wrong because they put a lot of effort and research into matching their brand image with the passersby they want to draw in. Imagine seeing the typical Victoria's Secret storefront, but when you stepped inside you found Maidenform lingerie. Whom do you think Abercrombie and Fitch is trying to draw into their store with shirtless boys standing outside their stores? Young girls and guys who are athletic and buff—and those who want to be. I know it's certainly a "Nope, not for me" store when I walk by. Ted Baker, on the other hand, now that's a store for me. Whether you have a brick and mortar location or are on the web, your brand is on display, being judged and evaluated instantly. Potential customers think you are meant for them or not, whether you and they are a fit. Once you understand your ideal customers' style, in order to use the secret language of style to your advantage, you need to understand the components of style: personality, voice, and price point.

COMPONENTS OF BRAND STYLE: PERSONALITY

FIRST AND FOREMOST, YOUR BRAND must have a personality. That's not to say to you have to create a character the way Geico did with the gecko, Aflac did with the duck, or Pillsbury did with the doughboy. They literally personified their brands. Then again, that's what Apple did so well with their "I'm a Mac" "I'm a PC" ad campaign a few ago. They personified the Apple brand as cool and the PC brand as nerdy. The list of companies that have personified their brands with characters goes on: Mr. Clean; the Maytag Man; the Snap, Crackle and Pop gnomes for Rice Krispies, and so many more. In fact, the furniture and decorative housewares store Pier One recently did an ad campaign with "style that speaks to you" where the inanimate decorative accessories came alive and spoke to the customer. Talk about speaking the secret language of style!

All this is very effective but it is probably not a strategy suited for many small businesses and entrepreneurs who don't use nationwide mass media. Allow your brand personality to come through in a more subtle and consistent way. Anthropologie is a brand that does this very well. All the stores have a consistent personality: a touch of romance, a bit of bohemianism, a large dollop of craftsmanship, and lots of creativity. Each store is unique, and they put effort into sourcing local craftspeople and companies to decorate the individual stores. So, while the brand has a global personality, they are also careful to capture the personality of the location of each store. They do brand personality brilliantly.

WeWork, a fast growing office-share company, also does this very well. Company-wide, WeWork exudes a personality of community, entrepreneurship, freelancing, and creativity. They also do a great job at adapting each location to the personality of its community. There are two locations within two miles of my home. The one closest to me, near the beach and a nearby marina, takes on a nautical personality. The other location, in the main shopping district, has much more of a cool urban feel. Clear personalities of each location are wrapped within the personality of the company overall.

As a long-time practitioner of yoga, I have some pretty bohemian friends. What I've always found really funny is how these anti-establishment, counterculture, don't-put-me-in-a-box friends, who refuse to wear brand labels because they don't want to be identified or labeled, have created another box for themselves. They often have a similar style. You know the look. A lot of hemp, baggy parachute pants, knit caps, beads, and bracelets around their wrists. I'm not criticizing the look. In fact, I quite like it. What I'm saying is, they are still wearing a label because the style is so identifiable. It fits their personality. Or as Creative Warriors podcast guest, Alan Iny says in his book, *Thinking in New Boxes*, "Thinking outside the box is just a new box."

So what's the personality of your brand? Humorous, classic, professional, casual? I suggest starting with five words that capture the essence of the personality you want to portray. Do these five personality traits complement one another and make for a compelling brand? If they were the five personality traits of a person, would you be compelled to want to know more about this person? Does he or she seem like someone who has depth and is likeable?

The personality of your brand doesn't have to be exactly who you are personally, but it shouldn't feel false either. For example, the brand image of my photography business is far more high-end than the way I live or desire to live. But it's a brand image that's authentic precisely because I understand the secret language of my customers so well. It's certainly a side of who I am and what I value. In order for the personality of your brand to come through, it has to be either rooted in truth and authenticity or completely made up like Geico's gecko. Either way, the personality of your brand has to shine through.

COMPONENTS OF BRAND STYLE: VOICE

THOUGH THEY ARE SIMILAR, THERE is a difference between personality and voice. Maybe somewhat ironically, the voice of your brand is more subtle. Whereas the personality of your brand shines brightly for all the world to see, the voice of your brand is a constant undertone.

Because the voice of your brand is more subtle, the easiest way to look at it is in layers. The style you are creating is like the outer layer. Under that outer layer are the layers of personality, voice, and price point. Your business probably also has "layers." Different services, product lines, income streams, or what have you, all layers of the whole, which is your brand and business. It all must have a consistent voice to be heard as a single language by your customers. In other words, you don't want to be switching languages, speaking French one moment and German the next. The voice of your brand is the most consistent part of the style of your brand. It must be inclusive in all you do.

The voice of our brands has to be authentic, clear, and comfortable. It doesn't come easy.

To maintain my voice while writing this book, I looked to the Creative Warriors podcast, my coaching style, and the Creative Warriors Unite website and Facebook group to "listen" for the voice that shows up across the board. How did my ideal customers—in this case, readers and podcast listeners—hear me? What I came up with is "I'm with you." I want you as the reader, to genuinely feel that I'm with you. If we were together, I'd be sitting across from you, leaning in, letting you know I'm with you every step of the way. It's genuine because I really am with you. I am a Creative Warrior; I have been since I was twenty years old. I understand the struggles, the emotions, and the strategies to succeed. "I'm with you" is a voice I try to be sure is felt perhaps even more than it's heard. That's a key distinction that makes the voice of your brand unique. The voice is almost always felt more than it's heard or seen. How am I doing? Do you feel I'm with you? I hope so.

The voice of your brand has to be wanted and appreciated and it must speak the secret language of your ideal customer in order for them to "buy" it. That is, to not only buy what you're offering, but also buy into the fact that the voice of your brand is genuine. It's best when it's a bit of both—what organically shows up and what you strategize.

Once you've teased out the voice and strategized how it works for your ideal customer, I suggest you create a visual. Can you imagine a scene in your mind, a movie in your head, that looks like the voice of your brand? In my movie, I'd be sitting across from you, maybe with a cup of coffee, leaning in, listening to everything you have to say. That's what "I'm with you" looks like to me.

What does the voice of your brand look like? If you were to direct it as a scene in a play, how would it go? This exercise is important because, with that visual, you can describe the voice of your brand to your team, subcontractors, and anyone involved in your business. You also know it clearly yourself so that you can be sure you are consistent with the voice of your brand. The voice of your brand as it pertains to style creates consistency. That's what it does best. With a consistent voice in your brand style and all that you create, your ideal customers will know you are the right fit for them.

COMPONENTS OF BRAND STYLE: PRICE POINT

As WE KNOW, THE SECRET language of style is all about helping people self-qualify that they are the perfect customer for you and to make a quick decision to choose you. We also want to be sure they are the customers you want! In the next chapter we're going to dive deep and talk about pricing psychology. But for now, we must consider how conveying your price point is part of the secret language of style.

It's rather simple, but often not done correctly. You'll know you're not correctly communicating the price point in your style if an inordinate number of people respond negatively when they find out your prices. They're surprised. Based on how you portrayed yourself, they didn't see that coming! Imagine if you went into your local diner for a casual meal and when the menu arrived it showed outrageous prices. Or worse yet, you found out how expensive it was when the check arrived! Have you ever had anything like that happen to you?

Sometimes consumers make assumptions. I would come across this occasionally as a photographer. Some people think a photographer is a photographer, and we must all charge roughly the same thing. But if they didn't go to my website or do a minimal amount of research, that's their fault. One look at my brand image and the people I photograph, and you know this is not going to be cheap. But for the most part, a business is responsible for the disconnect between what something looks like it will cost and what it actually costs.

Have you ever heard a customer say, "I don't know if we can afford that. It looks (or feels) expensive"? They may not know the price for sure, but are evaluating based on how the brand looks and/or feels. Consider the image your brand projects. Does it feel like your actual price point? If you were your customer, based on what you saw, would you be surprised by your prices? Would you be shocked it cost so much more than you expected? Or would you feel like it's a bargain because you expected it to be much more? Neither extreme is great, because you don't want push back on your price if it's more than expected. But at the same time, if someone expected it to cost more, you may be unnecessarily scaring off some potential customers.

However, feeling you got more than you paid for can be positive. You'll be more inclined to tell others about that product or service. Consider Tamsen Webster's brand favorite, Diane von Furstenberg. DVF has an interesting pricing psychology. With average dress prices ranging from $300 to $500, they are intentionally on the low end of the high-end. This is congruent with their overall language of "sharp and smart." You feel as though you are making a smart purchase and not paying an excessive amount of money.

On the other hand, looking too cheap can be a detriment. We've all heard the saying, "Too good to be true." Too low can make customers suspicious and actually deter people from buying because they assume the item is inferior. Given three choices, according to the "good, better, best" theory, with good being cheapest, best being most expensive, and better being in-between, most people will choose better, in the middle. People don't necessarily want the cheapest. Choosing the least expensive option makes them feel, well, cheap. You don't want to look so expensive that you scare people away. You want to look like and feel like your actual price point.

A great place to start is comparing how your style feels as to price point with other brands of similar price point, especially the brands your ideal customer is already doing business with. Whatever your price point is, high-end, low-end, or anything in between, make sure the style you portray is a close representation to your price point. Avoid surprises--unless it's a pleasant surprise.

YOU MIGHT BE WONDERING NOW how you use these elements of style—personality, voice, and price point, and where to apply them. Apply them to everything on the forefront of your business: your logo, font, signage, website, promotional material, marketing efforts, storefront, checkout process, invoices, social media. Style is in the graphics you choose and layout you create. Your team, staff, and employees also contribute to the secret language of style. The secret language of style is the decision-maker. Use these techniques of style to inspire your ideal customers to choose you. Make this your mantra—style to inspire.

⊛CH. 6

THE SECRET LANGUAGE OF PRICING

FOR MANY YEARS, I WOULD photograph families and children on the beaches of Nantucket, Massachusetts, one of my favorite places on earth. Nantucket is a small island about thirty miles by ferry off the coast of Cape Cod. With its cobblestone streets, gas lamps, and brick homes, it is a throwback to a different time. The town draws an affluent crowd who have summer homes there or are vacationing. Since I often needed to be there for an extended period, I brought my family along. My kids grew up thinking of Nantucket as their summer destination. Each year, we enjoyed a very special dining experience many times at a small restaurant called Company of the Cauldron. It was tucked away on a side street and had no sign. You would have no idea it was there unless someone told you or you wondered what sort of place had a large cauldron hanging outside.

Several things made dining at Company of the Cauldron unique. Of course, the food was spectacular, the ambiance was exquisite, and the harpist was special. But the most compelling part of Company of the Cauldron was that the menu simply listed the courses to be served—no choices to be made and no prices. They set a prix fixe menu a week or so in advance. Thankfully, or not so thankfully, I will eat anything.

It was a very special dining experience to simply show up and be served what was being served paired with appropriate wine. How much do you think dinner cost at Company of the Cauldron? Do you think it came cheap? No, it was definitely not cheap. What most conveyed the expectation that it was going to be expensive? Was it the ambiance? The harpist? The fact that the menu did not have prices tells you the restaurant was high-end. That's the power of the secret language of pricing psychology.

My very first experience in Bergdorf Goodman was eye-opening regarding the impact of the psychology of pricing. I went there believing I was a high-end portrait photographer for the area I was serving in my hometown. After all, I was charging $48.02 for an 8x10 print. Nearly fifty dollars may have been high-end for a market that was used to getting a stack of 8x10's from Sears for $19.99, but the message of my pricing was very low-end. My pricing was literally counting pennies. Two of them! The high-end market doesn't count pennies. Walmart has rollback pricing; other discount stores have very specific prices on their products, right down to the cent. They want you to know that you are not paying even a cent more than you should.

As I walked around Bergdorf's that day, I realized that how products and services are priced lets customers know if they're in the right place. If you can afford to shop in a place like Bergdorf Goodman or any other high-end brand, you don't expect to be nickel-and-dimed, so you won't see prices to the penny, such as $48.02. You'll see prices that are rounded off to whole numbers: three hundred, seven hundred, five thousand. If you're the right customer for Bergdorf's, one way you'll know you're in the right place is by price.

On the other hand, if you're on a budget or want to be frugal, seeing prices such as $19.99, $55.05, or $299.10, you are comforted that you're not paying a bit more than you should and you feel like you're in the right place.

That experience at Bergdorf's helped me realize the pricing of my 8x10 photo at $48.02 didn't make any sense. Not only was it a ridiculous amount, it also was a miscommunication. I was supposedly portraying my business as high-end, but the price portrayed a nickel-and-dime business. In this chapter, we'll explore how pricing sends a message to your customers—those you want to attract, and those you don't.

PRICING NO-NOS

WHY DO WE OFTEN SEE things priced at $99, $299, $497? This is because, psychologically, $99 seems cheaper than $100, setting a price at $299 seems cheaper than $300, and so on. Of course the precision of to-the-penny pricing attracts price-conscious buyers. If your ideal customer is not very concerned about price, be vague and emphasize service and the shopping experience.

The bigger issue may be that often brands overlook the negative impact of pricing just under a perceived barrier amount. If "affordable" is not the secret language of your ideal customer, that manner of pricing can appear unnecessary and clever. When "clever" is introduced into pricing, consumers get suspicious. Where else is this business being clever? Should I read the fine print? If being affordable or discount is the brand image, then by all means, price just below a psychological barrier. However, if your brand image is higher-end, then you definitely want to be straight and to the point.

What is the biggest problem when your prices don't match your ideal customer? You call forward the wrong customers, and they are confused. That's why the secret language of pricing matters so much. It lets people know they are in the right place and ensures you don't waste your time with people who are not the most advantageous for your business.

As you can tell by my own example, the biggest problem presents itself when there's a mismatch between the brand image and how products and services are priced. It's a complete break in secret language.

Bi-lingual is not a good thing when it comes to speaking the secret language of pricing psychology! You don't want to be speaking low-end with your brand image and then zonk people over the head with high prices! There are many places in New York City where you can expect to pay twenty-five dollars for a good burger. You don't expect that at McDonald's. Depending on where you live, a Big Mac is approximately $4.47. I don't eat at McDonald's, so I just Googled it. And yes, it varies based on where you live. McDonald's prices are not fixed nationwide. If you were drawn into McDonald's with their promise of a dollar meal and you found the burger cost $25, you would probably blow a fuse. Again, take note. The current price of a Big Mac is $4.47. Not $5.00. Not even $4.50! It's $4.47 in order to appear specific, affordable, and down to the penny.

WHERE STYLE MEETS PRICE

THE SECRET LANGUAGE OF PRICING is not only about the prices themselves, although that matters a great deal. It's also how the prices are presented. This goes right back to the secret language of style. Let's take the example of restaurants once again. As we already know, a menu with no prices conjures up a very definite feeling that the restaurant is high-end like the Company of the Cauldron on Nantucket. Imagine another lovely evening when you walk down the cobblestone street to yet another charming restaurant in a historic building, sided with cedar planks which have been weathered gray. The hostess seats your party at a table adorned with candles and fine linens. She pulls your chair out for you, and you settle in for a terrific meal. The waiter brings the leather-bound menu. You have your eye on a steak. On the menu, the price for the steak is "35." No dollar sign. There may or may not be a decimal point at the end. Convinced this will be a delicious steak and well worth every penny, you order the steak.

Days later, with your mouth still salivating over the steak you had a few nights ago, you decide to try another restaurant. This restaurant is more family friendly, so with kids in tow, you head to town. You're in a more hustling part of downtown, and there are street musicians. You walk past a musician, throw a tip in the guitar case, and step up to the hostess stand. You're brought to a nice table for four and anticipate a yummy meal. The waiter brings a large menu, which is great because each member of your family has a different idea what they want for dinner. Pasta perhaps. Or fresh fish. Of course, you decide to have the steak once again. On this menu it's "$35.00" presented with the dollar sign, decimal point, and two zeros. That sounds about right, and, when the waitress returns, everyone places their order.

The next night, you're in the mood for steak again. I know, it's getting a bit ridiculous. I mean, you're on an island, for goodness sake. You should be eating fish and seafood. But, maybe you'll have just one more steak. This time though, you're going to keep it simple. You'll go to a casual local hangout with live music that will occupy the kids and entertain you while you eat. The hostess leads you to bench seating, your whole family slides in, and the hostess hand everyone a huge menu. The pages of the menu are encased in plastic. You order the steak dinner you promised yourself, and a nachos and wings for everyone to chow down on while waiting for your meals. There's your steak. It's $34.99. Perfect.

You can see in the above scenarios the full range of restaurant experience from exclusive, to fine dining, to family friendly, to casual. From top to bottom, the price of the steak may have only varied by one cent. Yet the perception and the style of each restaurant varied greatly. From no menu, to leather-bound, to pages wrapped in plastic. So in this case, while the price itself varied the tiniest amount, how it was presented was aligned with the style of each establishment. Would you have expected to be seated without a menu and have no idea what the prices were at the family friendly restaurant? I doubt it.

Does your pricing style speak to your ideal customer? Or do you need to make some tweaks?

THE EMOTIONAL IMPACT OF PRICING

I WISH ENTREPRENEURS UNDERSTOOD AND applied the secret language of pricing far more than they do. Too often, businesses get far too hung up on the amount of money and don't pay enough attention to the emotional impact of their pricing. We blame the economy for hard times and fewer clients. While there may be some truth to that, it's easy for us to assume it's the economy and that the amount of money we charge is the issue. I want to encourage you always to look at what's underneath. What's the emotional impact of how your products and services are priced and presented?

Focus less on what the price is and more on how it makes people feel. People are emotional buyers. You can almost sell anybody anything if the reward is greater than the cost in their eyes. In their eyes. That's the key. From their perspective. A coaching client, Trish, who's a true superstar and confident in her quality of service, said to me once, "I can not only sell ice to an Eskimo, I can get them on a monthly subscription plan!" It's not about selling people what they don't need. It's about being committed to service and being confident in your abilities.

You need to approach the secret language of pricing with empathy and responsibility for the impact you create by the way that you price your products and services. You have a tremendous amount of control. Aligning the emotional impact of your pricing with the secret language of your ideal customer will call them forward and confirm that you and your business are the best choice for them.

THE SECRET LANGUAGE OF PRICING IN ACTION

IN MY PHOTOGRAPHY BUSINESS, I had the opportunity to experience firsthand the power of the secret language of pricing. During the transitional period when my photography business in my hometown was failing and I was just beginning my business in the affluent market, I literally had my feet in two different worlds. I had my place in Hopewell Junction, New York and had opened a new studio in Greenwich, Connecticut. That studio was in total alignment with what I had learned about the secret language of my ideal customers. Though the market areas were only a two-hour drive from one another, they were worlds apart in every other aspect. Not only was I entering the affluent market, I really wanted to work with only the best customers. I would offer a very high-touch experience and excel in customer service. Because I didn't want a high volume of customers, I would need to generate a high average sale.

How I was positioned within the Greenwich market was imperative. I wanted to be positioned as high-quality, custom, exclusive service, and comparable to other fine art in the home. In fact, I saw my "competition" as portrait painters, not other photographers. Those portrait painters were charging $10,000, $20,000 or more for a portrait of a child. I knew my rates had to be least half that in order to be positioned in the same ballpark.

A key phrase to remember: Pricing creates perception. You decide people's perceptions based on how you price your wares. I wanted to create the perception of fine art portraits with greater likeness than a painting for less than half the investment. For a brief time in the transitional stage, I charged $48.02 for an 8x10 photo in my hometown and $300 for essentially the same 8x10 in my new market. Yes, I made a number of improvements to the 8x10 in finishing techniques, but nothing that added up to that much.

My own example illustrates everything you need to know about the secret language of pricing. First, the amount. I was failing in my hometown trying to sell an 8x10 for $48.02. It was far too expensive for the market. Yet, I had no problem selling 8x10's for $300 in my new business. In fact, the affluent market wouldn't have had it any other way. Had I charged $48.02 there, my work would not have been perceived as high quality, and I would not have succeeded. The position you choose has to be aligned with the market. You have to consider the perception that is created. A too-high price might be unaffordable; too low is likely to come across as cheap. Price has to fit with and align with your ideal customer. Again, my $300 8x10 fine art portraits could have been cheaper, and I probably could have had an even larger segment within the affluent market. But I wanted the best of the best. I wasn't designing a business for everyone.

Next, my example reinforces the visual impact of pricing. For the business I was closing, I was marketing what was high-end for the area, but was priced in discount language with the very specific, down to the cent $48.02, which was a mixed message. I got it right in my new business, rounding off to a whole number of $300.

Thirdly, my example points out the need to get paid what you're worth. By what you're worth, I mean paid what will enable you to live the life you want. Otherwise, why are you in business? It's been said in various ways that an entrepreneur will work eighty hours a week for themselves to avoid working forty hours a week for someone else. I hope it won't come to eighty hours a week, but you will work hard. You do work hard! Your effort should sustain your lifestyle if not provide you with a life of prosperity, whatever that means for you.

Creation is a generous act. While creation may come from within, ultimately it is a very generous act to beautify the world with art, create products and services that make life easier, and, in one form or another, have an impact on the world, be it locally or worldwide. Make no apologies for your act of generosity and be sure you get paid what you're worth.

My personal example demonstrates the importance of creating a profitable business. I was not going for high volume. Therefore, each transaction had to be high-ticket in order for me to have a sustainable business. If you don't create a profitable business model, you may not be able to continue in your business. Then no one wins, neither you nor all the people who lost out on the opportunity to gain from your work.

Looking back, I'm confident that understanding the secret language of pricing and positioning myself correctly was the number one reason for my success. There's a good chance pricing will make or break your business too. This is not to be taken lightly. The good news is, is it's all in your control to decide how you want your business positioned in the market, the perception you want to create, and ensure that you are working with only your ideal customers to create a profitable business and the lifestyle you desire.

QUESTIONS TO HELP YOU IDENTIFY YOUR SECRET LANGUAGE OF PRICING

1. Do your ideal customers live like you, or are they wealthier or not as wealthy as you?
2. If you're buying something for a hobby or interest that you are passionate about, say a bicycle, handbag, or musical instrument, what's the top of the range of what you're willing to spend?
3. Considering your answers, what might be the range your ideal customer would be willing to spend on what you offer?
4. List three words to describe the perception you want people to have about your business.
5. Which of the following gives the feeling you want people to have of your business?
   a. 35
   b. $35
   c. $35.00
   d. $34.99

◆

PERHAPS YOU'RE STARTING TO SEE how each of the five components of secret language connect. As is true with speaking English, French, Italian, or any other language, when you become highly skilled in speaking that language, you have fluency. You can hear and speak the language as well as understand the structure, composition, and how the elements are interconnected. In the case of the secret language of pricing, the actual prices of your products and services let customers know if they're in the right place, and how they are stylistically presented confirms it. Fluency matters, and you are well on your way to becoming the master of your ideal customer's secret language.

⊛CH. 7
THE SECRET LANGUAGE OF WORDS

Now, you didn't think I'd write a book called *LINGO* without including a chapter about words, did you? There's hardly anything more foundational to speaking a language than words, right? But I'll bet, when you've finished this book, you'll think about the use of words differently when it comes to speaking your ideal customer's secret language. I want you to think about the secret language of words like cues you are sending to your ideal customers, as if only they can decipher them.

Consider the use of a lingo to bond a community together while separating themselves from the whole. Take teenagers, for example. Teenagers definitely have their own lingo. The words and phrases they speak to each other make sense to them and go right over the heads of their parents. That's the point. Their lingo gives teenagers a chance to communicate with one another and leave their parents in the dark. I found it amusing when I first joined Instagram, which is marketed to and used by a younger demographic. No one spoke in complete sentences. Photos that I post would solicit comments like "rad," "cool," and "dope," and included plenty of emojis.

In fact, if you notice, each social media platform has its own lingo. How you post on LinkedIn is very different from how you post on Instagram. Facebook has its own more friendly, "what's on your mind?" lingo. Snapchat and Twitter each have their own lingo too. Twitter's 280-character limit keeps posts short and concise. My ideal customer isn't on Snapchat (as of today), and neither am I. All of these social media outlets have their own lingo and their own demographic. That's the point of the secret language of words. Using words that express what you stand for, your values and what you do, stands out to the people who "get" you, and those who don't will neither know nor care what you're really saying because there's no emotional connection.

I said early on that the five components of secret language make up a sequence and must be built in order. First, you learned the importance of understanding your ideal customers' perspective. Nothing else matters until you understand where they are coming from. Then you learned how to stand out by tapping into their feelings of familiarity and comfort. Next, you helped your ideal customers' choose you because your style resonated for them. In the previous chapter, you let them know they were in the right place by understanding and working with their psychology of pricing. Now, you're pulling out the big guns. You're going to pull everything together using the right words to get the customers you want.

When I first started the Creative Warriors podcast, we had to find guests. The show was completely unknown. It was amazing that bestselling authors (and all-around superstars, in my opinion) Sally Hogshead and Michael Port were my first and second guests. Unbelievable! So it wasn't long before we had people contacting us to be guests on the show. Not having a large team, I was vetting the prospective guests to be sure they were a fit for the show. Why? Because I knew the show would be successful if we made sure every guest spoke the secret language of Creative Warriors. Having been a Creative Warrior myself for decades, I've got this down. I have a very clear idea what my audience wants to hear or needs to know about.

Today, I have a team to handle the several requests that come in daily, but when I first started Creative Warriors podcast, I had to check out the websites, blogs, and books of all who inquired about being a guest on my podcast. This was no small task. As I perused the websites, I was like a customer—with little time and even less energy to figure out what a guest had to offer. If a prospective guest couldn't convey their core message in seven seconds or less, I moved along. I know that sounds harsh. But do you think your prospective customers are any less harsh? If you do, then here's your first reality check. Believe me, until you have won them over, they have no reason to be kind. As is true for many of your customers, I was squeezing this work in between a million other things that had to get done. For me to choose someone as a guest, they had to make their message clear, stop me in my tracks, and be speaking the secret language of Creative Warriors.

One day, I came to a request from Tom Asacker. And there they were, front and center, placed over a cover photo on his website, six magical words: We become the stories we tell.

I had no idea what Tom did and no idea what his book was about. The cover was a photo of him on stage speaking at a TEDx event, which I hadn't listened to. But I knew in an instant that Tom would be a perfect guest. Why? Because I believe what he said in those six words. I believe that we do become the stories we tell. If we tell ourselves stories about being successful, we are far more likely to become successful. If we tell ourselves stories about our limitations and what we aren't capable of, we are far less likely to become successful. Those six words—we become the stories we tell—stopped me in my tracks. Tom and his website got a lot of my attention that day. I dove deep into his website, watched his TED talk, and downloaded his book. Of course, he was asked to be a guest on Creative Warriors podcast. Based on just those six words, I felt that I "got" Tom, and that Tom got me. Even more importantly, I knew that once he appeared on Creative Warriors, our listeners would have that same visceral feeling of being understood.

I was a customer, and Tom was selling a product or service. He wants to be hired to speak. Don't you think hiring agents who need a speaker like Tom would have a reaction similar to mine? That's the power of speaking the secret language of words to your ideal customer. You want to stop your ideal customers dead in their tracks, compelled to know more and to put aside any other concerns about price and competition because they feel they must have you.

I was so taken by my reaction to Tom's words that it got me thinking about why this was different from a slogan or a tagline. What was it about his statement that moved me more than any slogan or tagline ever has? It had an energetic quality. It was meaningful. It was said with conviction. My sense was that these six words came from a deep belief Tom held and were not just some clever phrase he thought up. Exploring the use of slogans and taglines became a technique I call Stand Out Statement™. You're going to read a lot about Stand Out Statements in this chapter—what they are, why they are so powerful, and how to create your own.

While the words we choose in our lives have various roles, for your business we're going to focus on three tactics that will be game-changers to market your business, attract your ideal customers, and assure that each transaction is worth it. It's what I refer to as Compel, Connect, and Clarify: Compel your ideal customers to pay attention to you, connect with them on a gut level, and clarify your message so that it's easy for them to understand what benefits and value you are offering.

THE POWER OF A SINGLE WORD

IT WOULD SEEM OBVIOUS THAT words would be an important part of speaking a language. But we hear constant chatter every day. It's very easy to overlook the power of a single word—even more so in marketing—and even more so when speaking a specific language to a specific audience. Every word matters. People get in the habit of saying certain things, a belief or a phrase, and it's become so habitual you wonder if they still agree with what they're saying. Businesses do this too. They get stuck using the same marketing phrases, the same words, and wonder why they keep getting the same results. When I went into business in the '80s marketing to the affluent market, describing my photography as "traditional" was effective. It spoke to the value of tradition and handing photos down from one generation to another. I was speaking the secret language of my customers at that time. But what feeling do you get today if I were to describe my photography as "traditional"? The word seems old and outdated! No one wants to hire the old, outdated photographer! They want the fresh, cutting-edge, spontaneous photographer. At best, I will say that my photography style "holds up over time." Meaning it's not a trendy style. I want customers to see the long-term benefit of their investment. But there's no way I would use the word "traditional" to market photography services today.

One of my favorite stories about holding on to outdated words is about Steuben Crystal. Steuben Crystal was an American company founded in 1903 in Corning, New York. In 1918, Steuben was acquired by Corning Glassworks. Many people know Corning for their cookware. Steuben Crystal, now known as the Steuben Division of Corning, became a high-end brand of beautiful crystal home decorative items. They opened a few very impressive retail stores, including one on Madison Avenue in New York City.

At one point in the early 2000s, Steuben ran an ad campaign in magazines, in the stores, and in other highly visible venues that read: "Steadfast in a Changing World." I understood what they were going for. They were making a point that they were maintaining a high standard with a priority for quality in the face of changing times and cheapening quality. But the moment I saw this campaign, I thought it was a death sentence. It felt very old, outdated— sort of like Grandpa digging in his heels and refusing the change.

Staying steadfast in a changing world is rarely a good strategy in business. Slogans more apt today would be "adapt to stay alive" or "reboot and stay relevant." But steadfast in a changing world? Ugh! Well, in 2008 Steuben was acquired by Schottenstein Stores, and in 2011, it shut down its factory and closed its remaining Madison Avenue store. Now, I'm not going to say the ad campaign did them in. But it certainly didn't help rejuvenate a dying brand during the downturn of the economy in 2008! The power of words to build and kill a business cannot be overlooked.

Another great example of the power of a single word is discount vs. upgrade. The words ultimately have the same goal, to give more value than price, but they are on opposite ends of the secret language spectrum. For example, it is unlikely your average Walmart shopper would be drawn to an upgrade. They shop at Walmart for discounts. On the other hand, the high-end market is all about upgrades.

One of my coaching clients, Kim-Marie Evans, has a blog for luxury travelers called Luxury Travel Mom. About the luxury traveler, she once said to me, "Give them free water and an upgrade and you've got their business for life. They couldn't care less about a discount." It's absolutely true! As a frequent flyer on American Airlines, an upgrade makes me a loyal customer! And I consume far more cheese than I should in the airport lounge. Why? Because it's a free upgrade! The entire premise of airport lounges is based on an upgrade. The impact of even a single word like discount or upgrade needs to be taken in consideration based on the secret language of your ideal customer.

COMPEL YOUR IDEAL CUSTOMERS TO PAY ATTENTION TO YOU

THE FIRST THING WORDS NEED to do for you is to stop people from whatever they are doing and take notice of your business. You need to stop people in their tracks. Or, nowadays, stop them from scrolling. This is why memes are so popular on social media. Instagram users love powerful quotes. Something in what is being said resonates with you and it gets your attention. It compels you to stop whatever you're doing and take notice.

In marketing terms, this is the top of the funnel. In other words, (pun intentional), you're less worried about qualifying the customer as the ideal customer for you and focusing more on what gets their attention. You can't have the rest of the conversation if you don't get their attention first.

But getting their attention is trickier than ever. There's so much competition for attention. Everyone is easily distracted because there's so much marketing noise. Attention spans are shorter, and everyone is in a hurry. And those darned screens scroll so fast when you swipe them. The real competition lies in getting attention. Entrepreneurs worry about the guy down the street or others in the same field, but your real competition is all the other noise that your ideal customers are expected to notice. As a society, we are all over the place, rushing from one thing to another, trying to live our lives. So many people we care about vie for our attention, let alone businesses trying to sell us their wares. This doesn't mean you have to be louder than everyone else. It means you have to be more compelling and more interesting than everyone else. If you were a tree in a forest, you'd have to be the purple one. As business author Seth Godin points out in his bestselling book, *Purple Cow: Transform Your Business By Being Remarkable*, you're either remarkable or you're invisible. To stand out from all the clutter and get anyone's attention, your words must be remarkable.

Let's consider for a moment the directional flow of your marketing message. Directional flow? What the...? Yes. The directional flow. Marketing messages that seem as if they are coming at the customer are usually blocked by the customer. We don't want to see or hear it, because the moment we feel we are being sold to, spoken at, or led to believe something, we resist. That's because it feels as though the business is focused on itself, telling us about itself and what it does. It's as if the business is walking toward people, which causes people to back up.

The opposite directional flow is getting potential customers to walk toward you. You do that by being compelling. Pique their curiosity and encourage them to want to know more. It's not hard to tell people what you do. You know what you do! The hard part is getting people to care about what you do. Creating compelling messages that get people's attention and inspire them to want to know more will help you stand out above the rest. There's a simple phrase I suggest you keep in mind—Compel, Don't Tell. Be interesting. Make them curious about you long before you begin to tell them anything about yourself and your business.

Here's where it gets magical. We pay attention to businesses that focus on us. If your marketing is not about you and you don't want to come across as selling or being pushy, then who is it about? It's about them! The prospective customers. Rather than tell them you are the right choice for their needs, you are going to let them figure that out for themselves.

Most people are pretty uncomfortable selling, so not-selling makes your life easier. It's easier to know what you do, but most people hate telling others what they do. It's harder to figure out what makes you compelling, but easier to get attention when you do. So I'll share the most effective way to be compelling and stop people in their tracks. It may take some work on your part, initially. But once you figure it out, you'll have a fantastic tool at your disposal to get the attention you need to stand out. A surefire way to stop people in their tracks is by using self-identifying questions. These are questions you are going to propose in your marketing that are compelling to the audience you want to attract, and probably everyone else will pass on by. It's as if the questions complete thoughts that are already running around in their minds, or offer a solution to a problem they've been thinking of, or plant an idea that speaks to what they value.

You will know you proposed the right questions when your ideal customers say things to you like, "It's as if you are in my head." When someone says that, it is the ultimate compliment because it means you have done all the work of *LINGO* to know someone's secret language. You started by understanding their perspective. You offered them comfort by working with what was already familiar to them. You presented yourself and your business in a style that matches their own. And you let them know they were in the right place by connecting to their psychology about pricing. So now, when you use questions in your marketing that cause people to feel as though you are inside their head, which is the ultimate acknowledgment of your empathy and the work you've done. You have just created the ultimate bond that truly makes you irresistible to your ideal customers. I get all verklempt just thinking about it.

Let's create some self-identifying questions I might use in marketing to you. It's a little tricky now because I've given you the inside scoop, but let's see if any of these questions resonate for you.

- Do you work really hard but don't feel like you're getting ahead?
- Have you reached a plateau, know you can do more, but you don't know how to get to the next level?
- If you could discover the one thing that will make all the difference in your business, would you want that?
- Do you know deep inside that you are capable of more, you just don't know what that is yet?
- Are you tired of feeling as though everyone else gets the attention you know you deserve?

When you read those questions, did it seem as though I was inside your head? Did any of the questions make you want to say, "Yup, that's me"? Those are all self-identifying questions I have used in marketing my coaching services. I know the secret language of Creative Warriors. I am one! Have been for many years! I have felt everyone one of those things and know that my ideal customer feels that way too.

Here's an example of one of my favorite self-identifying questions, which I helped create with one of my coaching customers. Bobbi is a successful photographer of newborns. The tricky thing about newborn photography is there's a very short window of time in which to photograph the baby, just the first two weeks after birth. The interesting thing about Bobbi is, although she doesn't have children of her own, she is able to completely understand the perspective of new parents. She's been photographing newborns for many years and she is one of the most empathetic and compassionate people you'll ever meet. Having three children of my own, I was also able to add to her perspective more information about what it feels like two weeks after a baby is born—aside from lack of sleep and smelling like baby vomit. The goal of coming up with self-identifying questions was to get into what it feels like as a parent of a two-week old child. What are they feeling? What's going on in their minds?

Here's what we came up with:

Has your world stopped, yet it feels like time is going by so quickly?

I can tell you from personal experience, that's exactly how it feels. The miracle of it all makes you feel as though your world has stopped. Yet, we all know the cliché of how time passes so quickly. New parents feel that way too. To get a proper newborn portrait, you only have two weeks! If you're the parent of a newborn scrolling through Facebook while doing a midnight feeding, if you came across an ad that said, "Has your world stopped, yet it feels like time is going by so quickly?" there's a very good chance it would get your attention much more than an ad that's waving a flag, claiming to be the best newborn photographer in town! Who cares? That would be about the business, which is not compelling.

For the parent of a newborn, an ad that reads: "Has your world stopped, yet it feels like time is going by so quickly?" would make you think, this photographer really gets me. The ad with the self-identifying question would compel you to contact that photographer.

There you go. This is the power of self-identifying questions to stop someone in their tracks, get their attention, and immediately make them feel like you get them.

Let's consider the process:

1. Know who your ideal customer is.
2. Understand their perspective. What are they going through? What are they feeling?
3. What thoughts are going on inside their head?
4. What question finishes the thought and offers a solution?

My recommendation is to start with several self-identifying questions. Then share them with people that you consider to be your ideal customer. Here's a very important catch: If you share them with people who are not your ideal customer, they will give you negative feedback, which is actually confirmation that you got it right. Your self-identifying questions should not resonate at all for people who are not your ideal customer. You can even test it by asking people you know are not your ideal customer. You don't want to start out doing that or you could get very confused and misled by the negative feedback. Just start with people you know share the state of mind and perspective of your ideal customer. They don't have to qualify as your ideal customer in affordability, location, or any other criteria, just state of mind and perspective. For example, Bobbi tested her self-identifying question with friends who had children. It didn't matter that the children were grown and out of the house. It's such an intense time for parents, they can probably recall the exact feelings they had when they had a newborn.

Once you've tested your self-identifying questions, narrow them down to the most powerful few. Now you can use them in your marketing, on your website, social media, online ads, brochures, car magnets, billboards, subway signs. Seriously, you can use them everywhere; everywhere, that is, that your ideal customers are going to see it. Handing out brochures for newborn photography in a retirement community is not a great idea no matter how terrific your self-identifying questions are. Using them on social media ads targeted at moms would be a much better idea. Years ago, I did a promotion for business headshots. I hired a young guy to stand at the local train station starting at five a.m., handing out brochures that said, "Are your social media photos more than two years old?" Asking a question with a specific time frame woke many executives commuting into New York City to the fact their profile photos were outdated. The promotion was a hit. Of course, because I knew their lifestyle, I stationed my guy at the station at five a.m. because that's when the Wall Street executives were beginning their commute.

Creating your self-identifying questions will be a fun, exciting, and, highly effective exercise. It's a blast getting into the minds of others! It makes you feel really good about yourself to care so deeply. So go ahead. Care deeply. Understand their perspective. Get inside their head. Have empathy and compassion. Enjoy the journey and love the results you see in your business when you easily get the attention of your ideal customer. Smile, knowing you just received the best compliment possible when someone says, "It's like you were inside my head."

CONNECT WITH YOUR IDEAL CUSTOMERS ON A GUT LEVEL

Now I'm about to offer you the magic wand. This is one of the things that I hope to be most known for in my work. Not because it's something I've done, but because of what it can do for others and how it modernizes something that greatly needs changing. It represents how businesses constantly need to evolve with the times, not only because time passes, but, more importantly, because of the way humans evolve.

I believe, as humans, we are constantly on a trajectory toward trusting our intuitions and instincts more. We're moving away from the logical side and more toward the energetic and emotional side. In an evolving society, we seem to be always moving away from leading only with our brains and toward emotions and how we feel. That's why speaking your ideal customer's secret language is so important and knowing their lingo it essential for the future of business. It is in fact, the evolution of buyer personas and avatars. Again, I am always grateful for the teaching of others that got us here. But what got us here won't get us to where we want to go. Where we need to go.

As humans, we are wired for primal survival, and it's important to understand that too. We need to see where old thoughts and patterns keep us stuck. To move forward though, we have to lean toward understanding the power of intuition. To succeed in business, we must understand that consumers are more likely to trust their gut and how they feel about a business than they have in the past. I predict that's only going to continue to increase.

That's why I'm going to help you understand the power of a Stand Out Statement™. The Stand Out Statement is the evolution of what has been called a slogan or tagline. For our purposes, let's consider a slogan and tagline the same thing and just call it a tagline. So what's the difference between a tagline and Stand Out Statement™? The difference is the energy that you feel from it. Stay with me even if this sounds "kumbaya." Remember Tom Asacker's statement that "We become the stories we tell"? I consider that a Stand Out Statement because of the way I reacted to it. It wasn't so much the words that were spoken. What mattered was how I, as Tom's ideal "customer" if you will, felt about the statement.

While this chapter is all about stressing the importance of speaking the secret language of words, in the end, it's not the words themselves that are most important. It's how the words you choose make people feel. This notion is best captured in the title of one of my favorite books by author Todd Henry, *Louder Than Words*. What's louder than words? How the words make us feel. It's the message and energy that is coming through those words. That's the difference between a tagline and a Stand Out Statement. Taglines tend to seem as if they are about the business, as if they are coming from the head, not the soul, of the business. A tagline might be super-clever but not create a connection.

The goal of the Stand Out Statement is to create an emotional connection with your ideal customer.

A Stand Out Statement lets the world know what you stand for, who you stand with, and how you to stand out.

Imagine, all that in a single sentence.

A Stand Out Statement is concise and to the point, made up of just three to seven words. Remember that goldfish have an attention span of nine seconds and humans have an attention span of eight seconds? That's why your Stand Out Statement can't be longer than seven words. You won't keep anyone's attention. That's a lot to accomplish in no more than seven words! Not only can it be done, you'll find that often the shorter the Stand Out Statement is, the more compelling it is.

Creating your Stand Out Statement is a process, a journey, if you will. So we start with what I call a Quest Statement. With the Quest Statement, you will determine the four essential components of the Stand Out Statement:

1. Your unique expertise
2. The ideal customer
3. Emotions of their challenge
4. The solution you provide

The solution you provide is a combination of how your ideal customers are feeling and how you can help. It's similar to the self-identifying questions that got their attention in the first place.

The Quest Statement is a fill-in-the-blanks format. So fill in the blanks of the following sentence:

As the go-to expert on [your unique expertise], I help [ideal customers] who feel [emotions of their challenge] so that [the solution you provide].

To put this in context, here's my Quest Statement:

As the go-to expert on speaking the secret language, I help uncommon entrepreneurs who feel frustrated they are wasting their time not getting paid what they're worth so that they can attract and keep their ideal customers and turn their businesses around.

Here's the Quest Statement of one of my coaching customers that resulted in one of my favorite Stand Out Statements of all time.

As the go-to expert on boudoir photography with a mission, I help women who feel ashamed if they're not perfect or think they have to play it small if they're beautiful so that they can love who they are-—just as they are.

The Quest Statement is not for marketing purposes. It is much too long. It is simply a tool to use on your way to your Stand Out Statement. It's for internal use only. It doesn't even have to make perfect sense or have perfect grammar. It only has to make sense to you and capture what you're fighting for. And yes, it should feel like something you are fighting for. In his book *The Entrepreneur Ethos*, podcast guest Jarie Bolander refers to entrepreneurs having an activist mindset. The Quest Statement should be who and what you are an activist for.

The goal is to create a business for you that you are passionate about so you feel excited every morning when your feet hit the ground, a business that you are willing to stand up for and demand you get paid your full value. It takes stamina and persistence to be a Creative Warrior, especially as you embark on something new such as transforming your business by learning to speak the secret language of your ideal customers. Trust me when I say it will get easier. With every win, working with your ideal customers, getting paid what you're worth, finding it easier every day, little by little, it takes a little less fight. Right now, you are on a quest. It should seem challenging. It only has to make sense to you and bring out the feeling of being a warrior on the quest of your life like a knight after the Holy Grail.

With your Quest Statement complete, you can start working on your Stand Out Statement. Unlike the Quest Statement, there's no set formula. Remember, the magic is in its energy. So now your job is to capture the entire essence of your Quest Statement in three to seven words. The essence. The feeling. The heart of the matter.

I sometimes refer to this as The Blurt. You know how sometimes you just blurt something out and it cuts straight to the point? You might surprise yourself. Whatever you have to say comes out completely unfiltered. That's The Blurt.

The biggest obstacle to capturing the essence of your Quest Statement and converting it into your Stand Out Statement is your brain. Your inclination will likely be to get too dramatic or profound. You're apt to get really wordy. On some level, you know you're creating something big and important, and your brain gets tied up in a knot. For your Stand Out Statement to have the energy that is required to make it effective, you have to get out of your head. Just blurt it out.

This usually takes so many iterations that you'll get really frustrated. Plan on it. It's not just you. Share your possible Stand Out Statements with people who could be your ideal customers and get their feedback. You'll get many blank stares, I assure you. Go back to the drawing board. You have to keep at it. When I'm working with my coaching clients, I shoot down so many ideas that they get pretty frustrated. That's when I know we're close. Chances are, as they get more and more frustrated, they will cut to the chase and blurt something out. Bingo! We got it!

Remember the boudoir photographer? Let's review her Quest Statement:

As the go-to expert on boudoir photography with a mission, I help women who feel ashamed if they're not perfect or think they have to play it small if they're beautiful so that they can love who they are-—just as they are.

Here's her Stand Out Statement:

BE UNAPOLOGETICALLY BEAUTIFUL

Just three words! See how those three words capture the entire essence of the Quest Statement? Her mission is to use boudoir photography to help women stop apologizing for who they are, whether they are naturally beautiful or don't carry the perfect body. It's all there in just those three words! It's a very strong statement, and women who have felt like they've been apologizing for who they are jump on board and say, "Dammit, I'm not going to apologize anymore. I am unapologetically beautiful!"

While almost all other boudoir photographers are telling people what they do, this photographer is creating a very strong connection with her ideal customers and inspiring them to hire her. It's as if joining the mission is more important than the photography. Because these women know that she gets them and they get her, a true connection has been made.

My Quest Statement:

As the go-to expert on speaking the secret language, I help uncommon entrepreneurs who feel frustrated they are wasting their time not getting paid what they're worth so that they can attract and keep their ideal customers and turn their businesses around.

Became this Stand Out Statement:

Freedom Fighter for the Uncommon Entrepreneur

CLARIFY YOUR PROMISE

AS IS OFTEN SAID, THE basis of any good relationship is communication. Once you have compelled your ideal customer with self-identifying questions and created a meaningful connection with them with your Stand Out Statement, now you can clarify what you promised and deliver an outstanding customer experience. It's your turn, shall I say responsibility, to be sure they have an exceptional experience with your business so they remain loyal customers and become strong advocates. Now it's time to use the secret language of words to clarify the core message of your business, assure them they made the right choice, and guide them through the process of your business.

When Tom Asacker's Stand Out Statement, "We become the stories we tell" compelled me, I wanted to know more. I wanted to understand where this idea came from. He piqued my curiosity, causing me to pause and dig into his website a little more—or a lot more. I wanted to understand why this was important to him. Clarifying is all about the customer journey from supporting their belief that they made the right choice to creating brand continuity with continual brand personality.

Once you've created the connection with your Stand Out Statement, your ideal customers may want to know more. This is when it's important to offer context as to why your belief is so strong. There's always a story behind a powerful belief and your ideal customers want to know what that story is.

In my photography business, we would include what we called a Care Card in every box of portraits we delivered. I have to say, this simple four inch by six inch card was one of my best usages of the secret language of words. It's primary objective was to explain to my customers how to take care of the portraits that were just delivered. But there was so much more to it than that, and it was one of our best marketing tools because it spoke to them.

At the top of the card was, "Things I care about. The well-being of children, education, the environment, abundance for all, and taking care of your portraits." That was followed by simple instructions about how to wipe off their portraits and to keep out of direct sunlight. The meaningful part, and what clarified what my business was all about, was at the end: "As for all the other things I care about, if you are involved in any charities or events that are in support of these causes, please let me know. I love to donate my services and support organizations doing good work."

This simple card generated a tremendous amount of conversation. Often I would find out about causes that are near and dear to a family because of personal reasons such as a family member who is battling a rare disease. This simple card deepened my connection to my customers. Often they opened up about why a cause was important to them and how it directly affected their lives. They took me under their wings and eagerly shared my work with their friends because I was eager to support them. Never, ever, underestimate the power of a few words to have a huge impact.

In fact, let's look even further into the impact a single word can have. Allow me to go all word-crazy on you. You can use a single word to personalize or depersonalize as you see fit in order to keep your customers emotionally engaged. At all times, you want to keep your customer emotionally connected to the product or service that you provide. It may also be advantageous to keep your customers detached. Not in any deceptive way of course! When you care about your customers as much as I know that you do, in their best interest, you want to keep them connected to the benefit and not caught up in the cost. Here's a note or email that might be sent along with the delivery of a product or service.

"Please find enclosed your invoice for the products you purchased. Thank you for counting on us and we look forward to serving you again in the future."

Sounds decent, right?

Here's a better way to write it:

"Please find enclosed the invoice for your products. Thank you for counting on us and we look forward to serving you again in the future."

The difference is in what you personalize and depersonalize. In the first example, the emphasis in on personalizing your invoice and depersonalizing the products you purchased. We wanted to personalize what is meaningful to them and depersonalize the expense, so we switched to the invoice and your products.

Use the power of words to keep your customers connected to the emotions that surround what you're offering and not distracted by the expense. Whatever we feel about almost all expenditures is temporary. You want people to reap full benefit of whatever you are offering. Select your words carefully to keep their attention on what serves them best. Depersonalize what isn't important in the long run.

Lastly, if what we are doing, creating, or offering, is truly unique, our ideal customers may not know the words to ask for it? This flies in the face of all advice to be Google-friendly and to have high-ranking search engine optimization (SEO). It's yet another example of "what got us here may not get us to where we want to go." For years, the importance of being searchable and to have high-ranking in SEO has been considered best practice. Not that it isn't, but what if what you do or what you create is so unique people wouldn't know how to ask for it.

Years ago I met a guy who had one of the greatest marketing challenges I had heard of. He's in the business of crisis management for the food industry. If a food product was tainted by a manufacturing issue or intentionally contaminated on the shelf, his company was called in to manage the potentially disastrous PR. As he said, if he did his job well, it never hit mainstream media. It was kept out of headline news. I replied, "If what you do is so confidential, how do you get more work?"

Imagine being in a business where you can't tell anyone what you did well. To do so would break confidentiality agreements and certainly not suit the next potential customer seeking confidentiality. His only recourse was to speak about the stories that did hit the media and say, "We didn't handle those." Truly one of the most challenging marketing challenges I've ever come across. But you know me. I love a marketing challenge!

I feel similarly about the challenging burden of responsibility to figure out how to communicate what makes you different without relying on what your customers expect. They only know to expect the norm. You want to stand out, to be anything but the norm. The norm is vanilla. You want to be pistachio. How would you explain what pistachio tastes like to someone who's never had pistachio? Kind of a minty, earthy taste? Sometimes it's our responsibility to create language that may not exist, to find a way to communicate what we do when what we do is unique and stands out from the rest. That is the goal after all!

SET THE TONE

NOW THAT YOU HAVE SELF-IDENTIFYING questions, a Stand Out Statement, and a clarified promise, you can use these and other secret language insights you've gained—who your ideal customer is, their perspective, what is familiar to them, and their style—to set the tone for the words you use in your business. That includes the words on your website, in your emails, in auto-responders, in thank-you cards, and in ads. Now that you speak their lingo, what is the tone of their language? Do they prefer simple turns of phrase, or are they intellectuals? Do they appreciate a no-baloney approach, or would they respond better to gentle coaxing and encouragement? Think of your tone as a person— would your ideal customer respond better to Judge Judy, Oprah Winfrey or Dolly Parton?

An excellent example of a company that employs a secret language of words to attract their ideal customers and deliver on their promise is Tumblr.com. Tumblr is a social media and microblogging site started in 2007. Its audience is primarily young, and the young at heart, and features a strong community presence. These communities are typically people in communities outside the mainstream—fandoms (people who follow a TV show, movie, book, or gaming series), for example. Tumblr knows this, and so it has branded itself as your quirky, supportive, positive friend. This sets the tone for all of the words they use. For example, when receiving notifications on your mobile device, rather than tell you that there's a post you might like, it will beckon you to check your feed by using blurbs such as "You'll want to be sitting down for this," or "You'll never guess what [username] just posted!"

Tumblr knows its audience very well. It will often give quirky error messages when the site has malfunctions: "We'll be back shortly. We may have forgotten to feed the wild Tumbeasts that roam our datacenter, resulting in gnawing and/or mutiny. Animal control has been alerted." They know what they can get away with and where boundaries are, yet they aren't afraid to push them. It's what makes Tumblr fun.

Here's another example. Lt. Col. Rob "Waldo" Waldman is a motivational keynote speaker, leadership expert, and *New York Times* and *Wall Street Journal* bestselling author. He also has one of the best branded websites I've seen, so I interviewed Waldo about the secret language of his ideal customers.

Like me, Waldo believes that consumers are growing more sophisticated by the day and they are constantly bombarded with generic messages, messages they see right through (or look past, as it were). "People are craving humanity more than ever," Waldo said. "So, it requires more effort to create a deeper connection with the customer."

Waldo creates connection by focusing on reliability, relevance, and rapport. He does the research to understand his audience and then looks for ways to make a connection with them. On Waldo's website, he uses military lingo such as "chair-fly" and "check 6." His book is titled *Never Fly Solo*. His military lingo is tied to his past service and also appeals to his ideal customers. The lingo differentiates him from other speakers.

It's important that everyone on your team—from your staff to your freelancers and vendors—knows the secret language of words as it applies to your ideal customer. Otherwise, you could end up with website or marketing copy that is entirely the wrong tone. For this book, I spoke with Thom Qafzezi, President and CEO of Molto Crescendo. Thom is an inspiring and results-oriented leader who transforms organizations through impactful mastery in executive and team coaching, organizational psychology, organizational and learning development, leadership development, and talent management.

Thom told me that he worked with a website designer who did not understand the secret language of his clients, who are senior leaders in the human resources industry. He told the website designer to look at his old website to get his voice down. However, she felt it was "too clinical" and needed to be "dumbed down," so she rewrote the copy.

"When I read the first draft, I knew it wasn't me," Thom explained. "I shared it with three leaders in the HR world who would be my ideal customer, and they described the copy as 'appalling,' felt talked-down-to. All of them felt that the copy wasn't congruent with Thom's business, that it was clear the person who wrote it didn't "get them," and one person said they were offended by it."

Here's an example of a change that didn't work. Thom's old website had a button that said "Services." The new web designer changed it to "Humanize Your Business." His audience is not going to take the time to translate "humanize your business" to "services"! She also changed "complimentary discovery session" to "free consultation," which is way too salesy. Most of her new verbiage was typical pitchy sales copy, which not only did not appeal to his ideal customers; it turned them off in a big way.

Take a look at all of your written communications with your customers and prospective customers. Does the tone fit who they are? Does it fit with their perspective and their style? Would it be familiar to them? Does it fit who you are as expressed in your Stand Out Statement?

◆

You now know the Secret Language Strategy. You know your ideal customers' lingo and you are better equipped to attract them to your business, compel them to choose you over competitors and other distractions, and keep them coming back. The next step is to learn how to use the secret language as you build your business.

P. S. Incidentally, Tom Asacker was a guest a second time on Creative Warriors and completely debunked his original theory that we become the stories we tell. We do, but that does not necessarily work in our favor. In his book, *I am Keats*, he explains how the mind gets hijacked by the stories running through our minds. It's a very interesting take on the idea and even more compelling to see someone challenge his original concept.

⊛CH. 8
THE NEW NICHE

IN THE PREVIOUS CHAPTERS, YOU learned why it's so important for you to discover your market's secret language. I'm sure that you can see now how speaking their secret language creates a bond and a feeling that you get one another. It's all about fluency, right? There is a smooth exchange of communication in speaking and listening. You also know what the five components of the Secret Language Strategy are and why we tackle them in a certain order.

Now that you can speak your ideal customers' language fluently, it's time to apply these principles to your business to create a culture. Think of this as building the "land" where the language is spoken.

For years, I've been saying something that may seem counterintuitive to many entrepreneurs: "Ditch the niche and diversify!" Why have I been saying this? Because creative thinkers need freedom from the shackles of a tightly narrowed offering and market. We're multi-passionate warriors and we don't want to be stuck doing one thing. It's not that niche marketing is inherently bad; it just needs to be redefined.

The traditional definition of niche is "a distinct segment of a market." It's also been used to describe the one thing you "do," your specialty. Niche marketing has been all the rage for years. Many entrepreneurs have claimed that it wasn't until they focused on one thing to do and one market to serve that their business took off. I don't doubt that's true. Yet, for a huge number of creative entrepreneurs that can feel like a death sentence.

In my community of Creative Warriors, we refer to following all our passions as chasing squirrels. I'm not saying chasing squirrels is productive. But I am saying the creative thinker is going to do it anyway. Rather than make them feel "sinful" for something inherent in being creative, why not figure out how it can be productive? We can make it productive by using the connections between them to unite the squirrels into a herd and then setting that herd off in a productive direction. We can cultivate a new niche.

The New Niche is not the one thing you do or the one segment of a market you serve. The New Niche is the space you own, or, you could say, the area of expertise for which you are known. Notice, I used the word "area." Your area of expertise can include many things, so it's not about the one thing you do. Space is expansive, even limitless as far as we know and so are the possibilities and the creative freedom you have when you become known for the space you own. When you or your business are recognized for the space you own, you gain creative freedom. With clarity about the space you own, you can diversify your business and create multiple streams of income.

The goal is for you to be easily found by only the customers who are right for you. You know your audience, your market, the people you want to serve. Now we want them to know where and how to find you. Note the language there: find you.

OWN YOUR SPACE

EMPOWERED WITH THE IDEA OF the New Niche, let's start by understanding what it means to own a space. In my lingo, the space you own—as a solo creative entrepreneur or as a company—is what you are known for. It answers this all-important, fundamental question: Of what will your ideal customers say you are the expert?

If you were strolling down the street, and you overheard the tail end of a conversation in which one person asked the other for a referral in your field and you heard, "Oh, [your name or name of business], she's the go-to expert for _____."

How would you fill in that blank? If you don't know almost immediately how to fill in that blank, then you don't own a space yet. See what comes to mind when you insert these well-known individuals and brands in that conversation. Fill in these blanks with your own ideas.

"Oh, Whole Foods, they are the go-to expert for _____."

"Oh, Patagonia, they are the go-to expert for _____."

"Oh, Seth Godin, he's the go-to expert for _____."

"Oh, Marie Kondo, she's the go-to expert for _____."

"Oh, Zappos, they are the go-to expert for _____."

"Oh, Geico, they are the go-to expert for _____."

"Oh, Rolex, they are the go-to brand for _____."

"Oh, Brene Brown, she's the go-to expert for _____."

Before we consider the answers to the above examples, let's first look at these three examples to illustrate an important point:

"Oh, Walmart, they are the go-to experts for _____."

"Oh, Bergdorf Goodman, they are the go-to experts for _____."

"Oh, Sears, they are the go-to experts for _____."

How would you fill in those blanks? Here are my suggestions:

"Oh, Walmart, they are the go-to experts for discount shopping."

"Oh, Bergdorf Goodman, they are the go-to experts for designer and couture brands."

"Oh, Sears, they are the go-to experts for… Wait… It'll come to me… No, actually, I have no idea."

That's the point. Does anyone know what Sears is the go-to expert for nowadays? I'm inclined to say appliances, but that was not the original intention. Without an easily identifiable space that you own, you flounder in no-man's land. If you aren't recognized for something, you aren't being seen and you're doomed.

Here are my answers:

"Oh, Whole Foods, they are the go-to expert for healthy eating and lifestyle."

"Oh, Patagonia, they are the go-to expert for an active lifestyle with environmental responsibility."

"Oh, Seth Godin, he's the go-to expert for provocative thoughts that incite change."

"Oh, Marie Kondo, she's the go-to expert for joy through minimalism."

"Oh, Zappos, they are the go-to experts for delivering happiness and exceptional customer service."

"Oh, Geico, they are the go-to expert for easy, quick, discount insurance."

"Oh, Rolex, they are the go-to brand for exceptional timepieces."

"Oh, Brene Brown, she's the go-to expert for vulnerability."

The New Niche being the space you own may be the single most important marketing strategy there is. On Creative Warriors, I interviewed Christopher Lochhead, one of the co-authors of the bestselling book, *Play Bigger*. In *Play Bigger*, Christopher and his co-authors refer to the idea of owning your own space as being a Category King. He stresses the importance of not only being the "king" of a category, but also being the first in that category. Being the Category King can certainly give you an advantage. However, for many entrepreneurs, it's less important to be first. It's more important to create a unique category for which you can be recognized and stand out.

HOW TO FIND THE SPACE YOU WANT TO OWN

YOU GET TO PICK THE space you want to own. That sounds really simplistic, but it's largely true—with two important caveats. The space you choose has to be marketable, and there has to be an audience for it.

But almost anything is marketable to some group. I met a photographer, Scott Bourne, who specializes in photographing wild ducks. I couldn't imagine there was much of a market for that. Was I ever wrong! With over 235,000 followers on Twitter, this guy has found a space that he is highly qualified for and it's clearly a huge market. Who knew? I certainly didn't know there were so many collectors of duck photos.

So I don't like to limit what is possible when it comes to the space you decide you want to own. The best suggestion I can offer is that the space you choose needs to fulfill the following criteria:

- It's something that you are passionate about.
- You are uniquely qualified.
- It's marketable to a large enough audience.

If this is a space you are going to own and be known for, it better darn well be something you are passionate about! To really dominate a category and "own" the space, your passion, drive, and commitment to that space must be evident and felt by everyone around you, including your competition. You want your competition to believe that you own that space so well they need to find a new lane because that one is full.

You want to find in yourself what makes you uniquely qualified to own your space. Qualification does not have to come in the form of education or degrees. Sure, that can be a factor. For me, in the space of coaching and working with Creative Warriors, it has nothing to do with education. Sure, the thousands of hours of coaching and leadership training I've received help, but what makes me uniquely qualified is that I've been a Creative Warrior for thirty-three years. I walked this path. I know its trials and tribulations. Plus, as a lover of observation, I have considered and studied every possible angle of everything that it means to be in business doing something uncommon. Look at your life experiences and perspectives that make you uniquely qualified to own the space you choose, and be confident in that. Your story and what makes you who you are qualified you far better than any textbook can teach. Own it, baby, and you'll own the space you want!

Your space must be marketable. But as I said, almost anything is marketable. It is a numbers game, though. If the market isn't large enough for you to derive the income you need to live your life as you chose, I don't consider that truly marketable. You want a marketable space that has a broad enough appeal to create a thriving business. Do some research. I would have said "no" to marketing duck photos until I discovered very large organizations like Ducks Unlimited with 700,000 members. So clearly there is an interest in all things ducks. It's not so hard to determine whether there's enough interest in your space. But I don't like to rule out what's possible until it's at least tested. I mean, who would have thought pet rocks or fidget spinners would have been all the rage?

EXPAND CREATIVE FREEDOM AND EARNING POTENTIAL

Owning your own space has other significant advantages. If you own your space, you:

- Have more creative freedom.
- Offer more diversity, probably appealing to a broader audience.
- Can create multiple streams for income.
- Make your business more agile to respond to future changes.

As you become well-established in your recognizable space, you are building a strong relationship of trust with your ideal customer. With this trust, you gain the freedom to create and explore new things. For example, Apple owns the cool technology space. We may not always know what to expect when Apple launches a new product, but we do know we can trust them to produce quality technology that is stylish— so much so that people will wait in line for days before a new product is available. Now that's trust! But think about the products Apple has created over the years: from computers, to phones, to MP3 players. I have no doubt there will be mass curiosity when their self- driving cars are launched.

Tesla is another interesting example. As car manufacturers go, they haven't been around very long. Yet they have developed exceptional trust. When they unveiled the new Tesla Model 3 in April, 2016, records indicate that within six weeks, 373,000 reservations were made with the required $1,000 deposit. That's $373 million in deposits, even though buyers had to wait months for the car to ship. Again, that's trust! I believe this high level of trust is not only attributed to the high quality for which Tesla quickly became known, but also because of the high profile of founder and CEO Elon Musk, one of the most admired businessmen on the planet. People are not only investing in the car they want; they are also investing in Musk's mission and the environment-saving technology. When you buy a Tesla, you're not just buying a beautifully styled and exceptionally manufactured vehicle. You are also making a statement and supporting a cause. You could say that Elon Musk owns the advancement-of-planetary-living space with his concern for Earth and his endeavor to colonize other planets. Owning this space has provided Musk and his companies to create cars, solar panel technology, battery power, and Space X. As consumers and observers, we grant him the trust and creative freedom to innovate.

With the creative freedom that comes with owning a space, you no longer have to shut down your multi-passionate ideas or shoo away those squirrels. It opens many opportunities for you to explore what makes you excited and what fulfills you.

With the creative freedom you've gained to create many things within the space that you own, you have also diversified your business. Diversification is great for your business on many levels. It certainly keeps your work day interesting. Diversification supports the creative thinker's innate need for stimulation from a variety of sources. There's no need to get bored when you have a variety of projects to work on in any given day.

Secondly, diversification broadens your appeal. Instead of having the pressure of getting one thing right to the right group of people at the right time, you have a far greater chance of hitting the mark with a diversified business. Different product or service lines may appeal to different audiences. Or maybe the timing of one thing you offer isn't right, but something else you do is in perfect timing. It makes sense that, with a diversified business, you stand a far greater chance to have something someone wants at any given time.

For example, when I started coaching, I coached photographers. They came to me because I was known to be successful in the field. But I soon realized the challenges they faced were not specific to photographers. Similar challenges affected anyone who was doing something unique or offering a different product. I saw that people need to do business very differently when they must connect on an emotional level in order for someone to want to do business with them. That is, when a business was more relational than transactional. My area of expertise became coaching "uncommon entrepreneurs," which opened the potential to coach entrepreneurs in many different fields—designers, podcasters, consultants, data architects, and some in fields that don't even have a name. But they are all doing something uncommon. They're all Creative Warriors.

Diversifying your business can also create multiple streams of income. This provides significant financial security for your business. Imagine your business with many sources of income. Not only can those sources of income come from a variety of products and services you offer, they can also fall into different categories of income. You can have a diversified business model with time-for-money services income, scalable income, and passive income. Some money may come in from your high-touch higher priced products and services while you are "making money as you sleep," as they say. I'll be the first to say there's nothing passive about passive income. It takes a lot of work upfront, but yes, eventually, you can make money while you sleep.

Your multiple streams of income don't have to come from a diversified business model. You can also offer choices within a single service. Multiple streams of income can also help even out cash flow if your business is seasonal. By owning your space and being identifiable for that space, you have gained the creative freedom to diversify and create multiple streams of income.

We all know how quickly things change in the world of business. At any moment, a technology can come along that will compete with our business, if not make what we do completely irrelevant. When you own your space and have diversified within that recognizable space, you are free to stop what doesn't work any longer and still have other options that work well. It's a very scary to do just one thing and hope you and your business will always be relevant. You're pretty safe in the funeral home business. The only guarantees in life are death and taxes. If you're in any other business, the more you offer, the easier it will be to keep your business relevant.

To use Apple as an example again, they are able to be agile, move into the area of self-driving cars, and position their business for what will undoubtedly be a huge industry in the future. When the space you own is clearly defined, it's amazing how much freedom you have to move around within that space while retaining the relationship of trust you have with your ideal customers.

TRADITIONAL NICHE MARKETING IS ALL about narrowing down. Do one thing for one group of people. You're left with a very narrow target; you better not miss. The New Niche is about expansion. Once you are known for your area of expertise, you can probably identify several other audiences. Think, "Who would love that?" In your New Niche, the thought will occur to you, "and you know who else would love that..." and, "oh wait, and you know who else would love that?" More than one audience will benefit from what you do and you can serve them in more than one way.

Your colleagues may tell you that niche marketing is the way to go, and I realize that it can be scary to go against the status quo. But you've already done the bulk of the work you need to do to be able to claim your space—your limitless, beautiful, fun, interesting, profitable space. Most people who focus on niche marketing stop at the niche, and never learn the secret language of their ideal customers. You've done that work, and now you can play with any number of ideas within your space. You're ahead of the game, my friend!

⊛CH. 9
CREATING A STAND OUT BRAND

WHY DOES BRANDING OFTEN GET a bad rap? Is it because people don't know what it is? Is it because there are so many different definitions? Does it somehow seem like the shallow side of business because it's about "image?" I have to say, I don't get it. I love branding! As I define it, branding is the visual representation of the secret language you use to communicate with your ideal customers. In many ways the brand image is the conversation.

After all the work you've done to learn the secret language of your ideal customers, what could be better than actually conversing with them? The goal of the brand image that you are going to create is to speak clearly to only your ideal customers, letting them know what you stand for, the values you share, what you are the expert in, and that you "get" them. You know you got it right when your brand resonates for your ideal customers and means nothing to those who aren't. It's true fluency—when you are able to have a two-way conversation that is shared by both parties: your business and your ideal customers.

Brand image is like the megaphone of the language you are speaking. Secret language branding is the communicator of the secret language to your ideal customers when you're not present. It's there when you are present too! But you know you've got good branding when it's speaking on your behalf, and you're not there. That's important today because so often, you're not there when potential customers are checking you out. Potential customers come across your business online or are referred to you. They may notice your advertising on social media, print ads radio spots. There are simply so many opportunities for people to come across your business when you're not there. Your branding better be doing you justice and speaking the right language to the right people.

My goal for this chapter is to not only make you passionate and excited about branding, but to encourage you to own your brand as you never have before.

TWO SECRETS ABOUT BRANDING

WE KNOW EACH OTHER WELL enough by now that I can reveal two secrets to you.

The first is that I have an ulterior motive in encouraging all this soul-searching work with my coaching customers in pursuit of their "why" and their authenticity. While it sounds nice and all, what I'm really digging for is to find out what makes them different. Research shows that 99.9 percent of our DNA is exactly the same. That means there's just 0.1 percent that separates us. That's what I want to find with you—the 0.1 percent that makes you unique. But the unique that I want you to find is not necessarily what makes you different. Pink hair, outlandish style, and body piercings can certainly bring out what makes you different. Nothing wrong with that! But it's not the most important uniqueness that I want you to look for. That 0.1 percent difference in your DNA is your unique perspective.

Have you noticed how siblings growing up in the same house can have a very different perspective on their childhood and family events? Maybe you can't get along with someone because they have such a different perspective on life, world events, or politics. You wonder how they could see things so differently. I think it's virtually impossible for any two people to have exactly the same perspective.

Your perspective is a combination of what I call the three I's: Impressions, Involvement, and Interactions. Impressions are how you interpreted things, perhaps from earlier years. You see things a certain way because of the impression they made on you. Involvement is how you've lived your life up to this point. It's how you've been involved in life from your education, career path, relationships, and so on. Interactions describes how things outside of yourself such as community, environment, and others have an effect on your perspective.

Now, if you consider all the things that have made an impression on you, favorably and negatively, plus the one-of-a-kind journey you've been on in life, plus the affect others have had on you throughout your life, you can imagine no two people could possibly have the same perspective. So, your perspective on life and your profession is one of a kind. That's the unique you want to find. That's your 0.1 percent difference. Once you discover that difference, build a stand-out brand around it that separates you from everyone else and speaks the secret language of the people you want to work with and that points out your unique perspective. So, the first "secret" I'm sharing with you is that, although it may look as if you are on a personally fulfilling journey of self-discovery, the real objective is to find what makes you different that can be branded. What makes you different makes you marketable.

The second "secret" is possibly the number one hack to success. After years of coaching entrepreneurs and hundreds of podcast interviews, I've observed that the difference between those who are successful and those who haven't broken through is how deeply they embody their brand and how clearly they communicate their brand message.

When I interviewed bestselling author and branding guru Sally Hogshead for the second time about her book, *Fascinate: How to Make Your Brand Impossible to Resist,* we had a terrific conversation about owning your brand. I brought up to Sally that I had seen her on stage at an event where she said, "The world is not changed by people that sort of care. The world is changed by people who passionately, irrationally care." In the context in which she said it, she was not talking about branding.

She was encouraging the audience as individuals and inspiring everyone to take action. But to me, there was a valuable branding lesson in that. If your brand image is "sort of" there, your ideal customers don't know what you stand for and whether they are right for you. If you want a successful business and to work only with the customers who are right for you, then you need a brand image that passionately, almost irrationally, shows up. There can be no mistaking what your brand is all about and who you are for. And you need to passionately, irrationally care about those you will serve or are building a product for.

WHAT SHOULD BE INCLUDED IN YOUR BRAND IMAGE?

LET'S GO OVER EACH ELEMENT that should be included in your brand image:

- All elements should feel familiar to your ideal customer.
- Your brand image should be in a style that resonates with your ideal customer.
- Your brand image should indicate your price point.
- Your Stand Out Statement draws in your ideal customer.

Elements that feel familiar to your ideal customer could include your choice of font, the name itself, and a design element such as a logo. Font choice has a large impact on familiarity. For example, you wouldn't want to appeal to a sophisticated market with a handwritten-style font. Just look at how different the names below feel because of the font choice. Imagine you're an interior decorator specializing in upscale, ocean-front properties.

Oceanside Fine Interiors

Oceanside Fine Interiors

OCEANSIDE FINE INTERIORS

Oceanside Fine Interiors

The change of font alone gives a very different feeling about who your business serves. Serif fonts indicate a traditional style with an eye for detail and often imply established and high-end decor. Sans serif fonts tend to look more modern and clean. It may not indicate as well what market you're appealing to, but other elements can make that clear. The clean, simple font feels sophisticated and speaks of good taste. Fonts like Comic Sans or handwritten give a feeling of casualness and seem kitschy and perhaps outdated.

Fonts can be trendy and come in and out of fashion. It's important to choose a font that will hold up over time. Let's face it, we've all seen outdated fonts! Please, for the love of all that is good in the world, stop with the Papyrus! To create a feeling of familiarity, choose fonts that speak directly to your ideal customer: sophisticated for sophisticated, formal for formal, casual for casual. You get the idea. But you'd be surprised how often I see businesses use a mismatched font to try to speak to a particular customer.

Your business name itself is part of your branding that should feel familiar to your customer. I mentioned that originally my photography business name was not my actual name. It was Light Images. Clever, right? Photography equals images made with light. But, after my first visit to Bergdorf Goodman, it was obvious that designer names were revered.

I changed my business name to Jeffrey Shaw. On my business card, there was a diamond-shaped "period" at the end of my name. When I was changing my business name, I was working with an elderly graphic designer. Not understanding the high-end market I was striving for and what I learned at Bergdorf Goodman, he kept insisting that that my business name should be Jeffrey Shaw & Associates or Jeffrey Shaw Photographers. He felt strongly that I would want to grow and include other photographers. I was clear that I was building a personal brand that would offer highly personalized service.

In a moment of frustration, I said to him, "It's Jeffrey Shaw, period!"

To mock me, he created a design that was just my name with a period at the end. I loved it! The period would always be a reminder of my mission—that it was just me. No fuss, no fluff. Just me. Period. I told him to change the period to a diamond shape. Why? I'll bet you can guess by now. The diamond shape speaks money. Don't you agree?

For my current business card for my coaching, speaking, and podcast, the diamond tradition continues, as does the mission to be clear, concise, highly personalized, and just me. When the brand image is right, it can adapt with the times, and still hold its meaning.

Let's look at another example of incredible brand change. Most people under the age of thirty would never imagine what Abercrombie & Fitch used to be. Abercrombie & Fitch, the clothing retailer best known today for its highly sexualized image appealing to teens and tweens, was originally a sporting goods store. At the original Abercrombie & Fitch, you would find tweed blazers allegedly the same as those worn by the likes of Ernest Hemingway and Teddy Roosevelt. In the early 90s it did a complete brand image change to become the hormone-induced environment it is today. Now that's a brand image that shows no remnants of its original brand. But it's a great example of how brand image can swing to appeal to a different market.

Another interesting thing about Abercrombie & Fitch is that the name still works. It sounds pretty traditional. The double-barreled name is reminiscent of the more formal business it originally was, like Smith & Wesson. The multi-name format will typically give a feeling of being well-established with a long history. You can use that intentionally too! I know brands that have combined made-up names in order to portray a feeling of having been long-established.

Once again, you want your business name to be aligned with your ideal customer. Using your own name, or even a made-up name that still implies an individual will always convey a feeling of custom and personalized and probably high-end as well. Of course, you can make up a business name. Just be sure it really feels aligned with your ideal customer. Don't be cutesy unless that appeals to the customer you want. It's called The Dollar Store for a reason, right?

When considering how your brand image will be on display on your website, business card, promotional materials, packaging and many other things, you also want to consider what style will resonate with your ideal customer. Is their preference traditional or contemporary? Clean or cluttered? Cool tones or warm tones? Formal or casual? Even though your brand image style is most often communicated online these days, still think of it as walking into a brick and mortar store. You know you get different feelings from differently styled establishments. A buffet restaurant feels very different from a steak house.

Style is all about decision. People make a decision, and a quick one I might add, based on whether it's "their style." Flipping through websites is a lot like flipping through shirts or blouses on a clothing rack. You zip through the hangers until one pops out at you. Why? Because of the style. Maybe it's the fabric, the color, or the cut. You are putting yourself at a huge advantage of being chosen over everyone else by your ideal customer if you replicate their style they choose in other areas of their lives.

Brand image style is where I have seen the biggest breaks in communication with businesses that I've coached. They want to reach a certain audience, but their brand image says something very different. To create an effective brand image that is perfectly aligned with your ideal customer, you probably have the least leeway when it comes to style, because you truly want to make it easy for them to choose you. So make sure the way your brand image looks, layout and all, makes your ideal customer say, "That's for me. That's my style."

Now, this is key if you want to attract your ideal customers. If you want to make your life much easier, your brand image must indicate your price point. It doesn't matter whether your price point is high-end, low-end, or meant for a mass market; your brand image must feel like what people can expect. Why does this make your life easier? Because, if your brand image doesn't indicate your price point, you'll attract the wrong people and waste a lot of your time. If you spend a lot of time justifying your prices, I strongly encourage you to look at your brand image. If you're expensive, look expensive. Don't be afraid it will scare people off. That's the point! You are not for everyone. On the other hand, be sure you don't look exclusive if you're not. Of course, people won't know exactly what they are going to spend by looking at your brand image. But it must give them an indication. If it doesn't, you can be assured you are not going to attract the customers who are right for you.

The last element that must be included with your brand image is your Stand out Statement because, well, this is everything. As discussed in Chapter 7, this three- to seven-word sentence is the direct line of communication between your business and your ideal customer. More than anything else, this magnetizes your ideal customer and filters out the rest. It makes you stand out above the noise so that, to your ideal customer, you simply make sense.

You've captured their attention with your Stand out Statement and compelled them to want to know more. That's exactly what creating a stand-out brand image is supposed to do. Be sure you include your Stand out Statement on everything. It should be front and center on your website, highlighted on promotional materials, used in advertising. With your Stand out Statement speaking loudly on your behalf as part of your brand image, you are almost guaranteed to attract only your ideal customers.

I HOPE I'VE MADE A strong case for why brand image is important. It's not shallow because it's about "image." It's about creating a connection. Brand image is not just for big companies. It's is about heart and soul, which is more easily conveyed by entrepreneurs and small businesses. Creating the right brand image is not just another thing to do. It's the one thing that holds everything together. It's not complicated. It's simple—it's the outward projection of the secret language of your ideal customers that you've worked so hard to speak. Speak it loud, proud, and clear.

✱◯CH. 10
BUILDING A COMMUNITY

THE PARETO PRINCIPLE, KNOWN AS the 80/20 rule, states that 80 percent of your business comes from 20 percent of your customers. One of the best ways to beat the Pareto Principle so that all your customers are the right customers is to create a community of loyal customers. You want to create an expansive, but tight, circle of customers, people who keep coming back and refer your business to their friends.

I'm just going to say it. We don't talk enough about love in business. Yes, love. One of the best ways to build a community of loyal customers is by loving them. As I wrote in the introduction, one of the pivotal moments for me as a parent was when I read the book, *The 5 Love Languages*. In his classic book, Gary Chapman identifies five ways people feel love: words of affirmation, physical touch, gifts, quality time, and acts of service. My eldest son was a match for what I thought my role was as a father: to praise and build up his self-esteem. Providing words of affirmation came naturally to me and, fortunately, that was how he received love. My two daughters each responded to feeling love differently. Words of affirmation did not have the same positive impact and did not conjure up feelings of love for them. As it turns out, my oldest daughter felt love when I spent quality time with her. My youngest daughter responded best to physical touch.

This parenting lesson taught me a great deal about business and speaking the language of love to my customers. It also introduced an interesting paradox. What made each of my children feel loved was one of five languages. Not ten, not fifty, not hundreds. One of five. I was catering to what love felt like to each of them, yet that was only one of five choices. The same thing is true in speaking the secret language of love with your customers. When you are speaking the correct secret language of your ideal customers, generalizations can be made about them as a community, without judgment, assumptions and stereotypes. You don't have to adapt your cadence for each of them individually, yet you can make each of them feel as if you are only speaking to them. Because your ideal customers share some values (which you used to identify them in the first place), you can find some common verbiage, even if there are differences—sort of like the differences between French in France and French in Quebec.

If there was ever a chance for entrepreneurs and small businesses to win out over big business, it is in the ability to speak the secret language of love with their customers. We can be right in there with them, listening for what is being said and for what isn't being said but is needed. We can pivot on a dime and adapt our businesses and experiences. We can add personal touches that feel like love to our ideal customers, touches that inspire them to gush over us by coming back time and again and telling their friends about us. That's how you build community and that's how you create loyalty.

Three primary areas of concentration help you create amazing loyalty for you and your business:

- Grow a community.
- Identify their deeper need.
- Let them have an experience.

FUNDAMENTALS OF GROWING A COMMUNITY

RIGHT OUT OF THE GATE, there's something I'd like you to change immediately. I think you get the point by now that language matters, correct? The words you speak have an impact on others. But equally important, the words you hear yourself speak have an impact on your own perspective and behavior. For example, in my business we don't have a marketing plan, we have an enrolling plan. Every time I hear myself speak about our enrolling plan I am reminded of the responsibility we have to build relationships that inspire people to walk toward us, to enroll them into service that I wholeheartedly believe will help them as opposed to a plan to market at them.

We also speak about impact more than budgets. The truth is, and evidence has shown, that money always follows impact. The greater the impact we can create, the more opportunities follow. I highly encourage you to get as picky as I am about the words you hear yourself speak. Your words are training your brain at all times. I encourage you to not speak about the people your business serves as a target audience to be hit, an audience to speak at, consumers to swallow whatever you're dishing out, or a database. If you speak about them in such distant, non-personal terms, they will feel that.

What you are building is a community, not accounts that pay you, do business with you, or are names on an email list. You are building a community of followers linked together by common threads of lifestyle and values. They are each beautifully unique, yet there are commonalities. If everyone in your community were to meet, large and small, you would expect they would "get" each other. This mindset of community ups the ante on how you relate to those your business serves. It increases the level of responsibility to build trust and maintain a high level of integrity. Is it more work? Does it carry a bigger burden of responsibility? Absolutely! But if you want to get off the proverbial hamster wheel and build a community that rewards you for years to come, it's well worth stepping up and taking the responsibility.

As an additional bonus, if you look further down the road at when you might sell your business or perhaps seek sponsors or collaboration with other businesses, your influence over a dedicated community has huge value. Other businesses will be anxious to partner with you or if you influence a community that they too want to reach. You own a space, and others want in.

Although I often look at how other businesses and pop stars are building communities today, perhaps the greatest example of community ever built was around The Grateful Dead. I'll be honest, without Googling, I don't think I can name a single Grateful Dead song. Sorry all you Deadheads! But that's my point. They did such a phenomenal job building a community that, even if you're not part of it, you know what The Grateful Dead is!

Many recent pop stars have done a fantastic job at creating strong communities of their own. One of the greatest at building a community in recent years is Lady Gaga. While Lady Gaga has explored many genres of music from performing with classic crooner Tony Bennett to a touch of country in her album, *Joanne*, her core community of Little Monsters continues to drive her success. Along the way in developing her community came the Monster Claw hand gesture, a Facebook-like social network that only her most loyal fans know about, and even innovation in perfume as the first fragrance to spray black and turn clear upon contacting the skin. To stay on brand and aligned with her community, she insisted on that innovation when the Cody company approached her. If you're interested in learning more about Lady Gaga's marketing prowess, check out my interview with Jackie Huba, author of *Monster Loyalty: How Lady Gaga Turns Followers into Fanatics* on the Creative Warriors podcast.

Other pop stars who also build communities include Taylor Swift with her Swifties and Justin Bieber and his Beliebers. But building communities is not relegated to pop stars. Author and Creative Warriors podcast guest Eddie Yoon refers to what he calls "Super Consumers." There's a good chance we're all super consumers of something, a product, service, or business that you have a strong allegiance to. Eddie defines a super consumer as someone who cares a great deal about a particular category, product, or service and who cares so much about it price is less of an issue.

Anyone who has a daughter probably got swept up in being a super consumer of American Girl dolls at some time. There are certainly cheaper dolls, but these young girls, and by proxy their families with credit cards in hand, become super consumers because rarely is one enough. It's impossible to avoid talking about Apple when it comes to super consumers. A frenzy is created whenever a new product is launched and, as we know, one is never enough. Back in the day, when you saw someone buy their first Apple product, you wished them luck because you knew they were hooked. Super consumers of wine devote a lot of time to being educated about wine to make the best selection and the expense is less of an issue. Harley-Davidson is another company that certainly has a devoted base of super consumers who are very loyal to the brand and spare almost no expense for their Harley lifestyle.

What are you a super consumer of? Is there something that you care about more than most people and probably spend more money on? It could be a hobby or a luxury you can't imagine being without. I'm a super consumer of chai tea. Not just any ol' chai tea. The real deal—loose black tea with cardamom, cinnamon, cloves, and ginger that I steep in boiled milk and pour through a strainer as part of my morning routine. I go to great lengths to drive to a specialty tea shop to purchase my chai tea and spend as much per ounce as you might for precious metal. As to most any other thing in life, I can take it or leave it, but don't mess with my chai tea. That makes me a super consumer.

Think of the community you are building as your super consumers, the ones who are most devoted to you and care a little less about price. The payoff for you is as your devoted fans, your established relationship with them makes doing business together much easier. Easy is good!

You can take specific steps to create a community, such as starting a Facebook group, referring to your community by a specific name, and bringing your community together at a live event, as I've done with the community of Creative Warriors. Many start as listeners of the podcast, join our Creative Warriors Unite Facebook group (www.JoinWarriors. com), attend weekly coaching calls, and come to a live event where we all can gather. I see it as a worldwide community of Creative Warriors.

If you don't want to go to the lengths of creating groups and gatherings, simply changing how you view the patrons of your business can go a long way. By breaking down the barriers between business and customer, you raise the level of interaction and sense of community. Whether your business is big or small, whether your customers are worldwide or local, you can create a community that holds your most loyal customers together. I guarantee it makes speaking a secret language much easier when you are speaking to a specific community.

Thinking of your business as building a community increases your level of care and responsibility. You can show love for your community through special offers meant only for current members of your community. Why have specials just for newbies? Knowing them as well as you do, you can express what's on their mind. That makes people feel they belong in your community and shows love.

IDENTIFY THEIR DEEPER NEED

NOTHING CREATES MORE LOYALTY THAN understanding your customer's deeper need. If you want to get to the heart of what makes someone feel like you "get" them, understanding their deeper need is the way. So what is a deeper need? I'll explain it this way. We all have layers of needs. You might be familiar with Maslow's Hierarchy of Needs pyramid which describes layers of needs from what's basic to survival up to self-actualization. In the middle of the triangle, the third layer, is love and belonging. We'll go into the need for belonging in Chapter 11. Right now, let's focus on love, the secret language of love.

What makes you feel loved more than someone knowing what you really need, something you may not even know to ask for? Have you ever helped someone going through a tough time? Maybe she's sharing her pain and all she's going through and just asking you to listen, but you know what she needs more than anything is a hug. So you give her a long embrace, her body settles in, and she's incredibly grateful because that's exactly what she needed. I'm not saying you should go around hugging all your customers! Although that wouldn't be all bad as shown in the book *Hug Your Customers* by Jack Mitchell. (As long as you ask permission first!) You can make people feel they are being held lovingly without touching them.

The "deeper need" is what your customer really needs but doesn't know or wouldn't think to ask for. It's the very powerful non-verbal part of the secret language. Have you ever looked at someone, spoken not a word, and yet so much was said? Or been so comfortable in someone's company that nothing needed to be said? Recall that feeling you get when you see a friend after a long time and it's as if no time has passed at all. That's this beautiful, energetic non-verbal communication. It's often more powerful than words.

When I was starting out as a photographer, my customers asked for what they needed: family portraits to capture this time in their lives, perhaps photos for holiday cards. Let's call that the obvious need. It's what they knew to ask for. Of course, I could provide that, and they'd be happy. But what if I captured something more? What if I addressed a deeper need that they didn't know to ask about? What if you did that for your customers? They would appreciate you more, it would create a tight bond, and they'd be loyal to you, For my photography customers, I understood they wanted photographs to hang on the wall, display on tables, give as gifts, and send on holiday cards. There were a few other things I knew they needed that they never asked for. I suspect no one ever will—until maybe now after reading this book!

My photography customers also wanted my assistance in making sure they were responsible parents. You see, because I understood the perspective of my ideal customers so well and spoke their secret language, I understood that, when you have money, all your kids have to be treated equally, right down to how many photographs there are of each child. When money cannot be an excuse, how do parents explain why there are more portraits of one child than another? They can't.

I'm the youngest of three boys. I have one childhood photo of myself alone. It could be that my parents were busier or bored with another son. It could also be that they had less money for such luxuries. As the third child, I tipped the scale, and they needed to move from the apartment in my grandparent's house to buying their first home. Certainly money was tight. In families where money is tight, there is some disparity in children's photos because sometimes you have money and times you don't. In a family of means, that disparity is not so acceptable. No customer of mine explained that to me. Knowing them so well, I figured that out on my own.

Similarly, customers didn't ask me to move them to tears when I photographed their precious children. Yet that was my goal. I wanted to accomplish far more than a photograph to hang on the wall. I wanted to stop them in their tracks as they walked down the hall, reflect for a moment on a time gone by, and shed a tear of joy and fond memory. No one ever asked for that.

Here's a more tangible example. With each greeting card order we gave a nice pen that closely matched the color of ink of the return address. I know how meticulous my ideal customers are. Their "style" is to be seen as being very put together by the hundreds of family members and friends who will receive their holiday card. Knowing that's their secret language of style, I figured they would run around town looking for the perfect pen so that the addresses on the envelopes would match the return address. No one would think to ask a photographer to supply a matching pen! But I didn't want to be just any ordinary photographer. I wanted to be the photographer they stuck with for years because I spoke their secret language of love and knew their deeper needs.

Is it a surprise that I had a super-successful photography business? I think not. And it will be no surprise when you have a successful business working with your ideal customers who come back to you time and again and who share your business with their friends.

How do you discover their deeper needs? While it would be nice, it's not realistic to think that you could cater to the individual deeper needs of every customer. But you can find some general deeper needs amongst all your ideal customers. You can generalize about the deeper needs of a large group of people based on their values.

We've already determined that what people value is a large part of their secret language. Values can be pretty consistent across a broad group of people. People of different generations value different things. Geographically different values are based on the culture of the area. Different socioeconomic groups have different values. While some value quality, some value price. If you imagine walking in their shoes and muster up all the empathy and compassion you have in order to understand what it feels like to be them, then what you discover to be their deeper needs will make sense. It may not be obvious at first, but it will make sense.

You have to understand their perspective in order to determine their deeper need. There's no other way. You have to "be them" and see the world through their eyes in order to sense what would make them feel like you hit their deeper need. Remember, they don't know to ask for this need. One way to unearth this unspoken need is to read between the lines. What is it that they are saying, but not really saying? For example, a coaching customer who's a family photographer told me that recently she's had several prospective customers say that they used to go to Sears for their family photos and now they wanted to come to her studio.

She went on to express that she didn't even respond to their inquiries because if they had purchased from Sears in the past, there was no way they could afford her. As a photographer producing high-quality portraits, she actually took offense at the comparison. She saved herself from wasting her time, right? But that's not how I saw it, especially since it had happened on more than a couple occasions. What might they be saying between the lines?

I suggested that a deeper need amongst her customers might be showing up. I asked her what kind of cars these potential customers drove. She said BMW, Audi, Lexus. These were not the cars one associates with spending a mere $9.99 for a collection of photos. If these car brands are familiar to them, what else might be? Though it seemed these folks might be frugal, having only spent $9.99 on photos in the past, clearly that's not the case.

My customer's assessment that they are not her ideal customers because they used to go to Sears was not accurate. I suggested that, between the lines, they were saying something very different. Perhaps, "we are proud of the fact that we used to only be able to afford Sears, but now we can afford a legitimate, professional photographer with a great reputation." Their deeper need was for the quality portraits my coaching client could produce to represent their upward mobility, to show that they "made it" and have climbed the ladder of success.

That being their deeper need, you can imagine that having portraits done is a big deal for them. They can afford it, but it's not chump change. Therefore, the photographer has to make it a big deal. First, I suggested she increase her prices since they actually wanted to overspend as a measure of their accomplishment. Crazy, right? But it's true. Second, I suggested the experience should be a big deal. The portraits session and the portrait-selection appointment should feature wine and cheese. How about an unveiling at the home when the portraits are competed? Make it a big deal, charge handsomely, make them feel better about themselves and all that they accomplished. Address their deeper need. Listen to not just what's being said, but what they don't say that's hidden between the lines.

The fundamental question you are trying to answer in order to discover the deeper needs of your customers is "what is it that they would most like to avoid?" Try making a list of things you think your ideal customer would most like to avoid. With my photography customers, it would be to avoid having to explain to any of their kids why there are more photographs of one child than another. They want to avoid the feeling of regret if they didn't capture the passing of time as their family grew. They want to avoid looking for the perfect pen to address their holiday cards.

Start now. Take out paper and pen or open Evernote and make a list of the things you think your customers would most like to avoid. Maybe they'd like to avoid feeling wasteful with their money, or avoid not having enough money by the end of the month, or heck, having bill collectors call them. That's a good thing to avoid! Then I'd say that customer is price conscious and has a deeper need to not feel guilty about their purchase along with an even deeper need to feel self-worth. Therefore, you would not only comfort them by making sure they know they didn't spend any more than they had to, but go a step farther and congratulate them on their prudence. Help them justify their purchase. Get them over the guilt and feeling good about their decision. Assure them they are worth it. Can you imagine how that would make them feel? Even more important, can you feel how that would feel? Make a list or do a brain dump of all the things your ideal customer would love to avoid. Keep it as a document or a poster on the wall.

Our deeper needs pertain to what we value. You can create a mind map of what you believe your ideal customer values. Draw a circle and put your ideal customer in the center. You can use a name that reminds you of your ideal customer or you can list their characteristics. Then make spokes, like sunrays, out from the center. Think of what your ideal customers value most, not possessions and things, but life values. What really means the most to them? Again, be them. If you were them, what would you value most? Write one of those things at the end of each spoke. You now have three techniques to discover the deeper needs of your ideal customer:

- Read between the lines.

- What are they trying to avoid?
- What do they value most?

Combined, these three techniques represent listening, empathy, and understanding. Now I ask you to consider this: Does anything make you feel better than being heard, felt, and seen? Can you imagine any better way to create a loyal relationship? Knowledge of their deeper needs may not come right away. But work with these three techniques, and some answers will become clear. They may not come easily at first. That's a good thing. What comes easily isn't as impactful. Your competition isn't taking the time to do this. That's why you'll stand out and rise above the noise. That's why your customers will keep coming back and will spread the word about your business—because you are speaking the language of love.

LET THEM HAVE AN EXPERIENCE

THE SECRET LANGUAGE IS ABOUT not settling for good enough. It's about going further than what's been done up to now and doing more than most people ever would. It's about not just knowing your customers, but being fluent in their language. The secret language goes beyond the demographics of avatars and buyers' personas to seeing the world through their eyes, to not just giving them what they ask for but providing what they don't know to ask for. At this stage of speaking the secret language of love and creating loyalty, we need to go beyond the norm of what is expected and what other businesses might do.

For years something has been getting under my skin when I hear people talking about creating experiences for their customers. There's nothing wrong with the topic. What's been bothering me is that there's something more that I don't hear anyone talking about. I wasn't sure what it was, and then, aha! It's a secret! That's why I didn't hear anyone talking about it. The problem about creating a unique—or great or whatever adjective you want to put before the word—experience, is that it's become cliché. At the root of the meaning of the word cliché is "common." It's a common, or trite, phrase. Well, you certainly don't want to be either trite or common! So sure, create great experiences for your customers. That's a good thing. Now, you can go even farther. This step farther will create the loyalty that you are looking for.

Instead of creating an experience for your customers, let them have an experience. Directionally speaking, it's no different than marketing at people vs. compelling people toward you, or allowing people to self-qualify and self-identify as discussed in Chapter 6. Instead of you creating the experience, you create the environment where your customers have their own experiences. The idea is similar to the principles of extrinsic vs intrinsic motivation. Extrinsic motivation is when things outside of ourselves motivate us. Maybe it's a sense of responsibility or discipline. Maybe it's the demands of someone around us. Extrinsic motivation comes from outside of us and kicks our butts into gear. Intrinsic motivation comes from within. It's when something deeply meaningful to us inspires us.

Extrinsic motivation is like dieting to look good while intrinsic motivation is changing your lifestyle to be healthy. The important thing is, intrinsic motivation sticks. When something is deeply meaningful inside us, to us and only us personally, the changes we make are far more likely to stick in the long run. The same is true with experiences. Experiences you create for your customers will be enjoyed in the moment and probably forgotten before long. When you let your customers have an experience, it will stick with them far longer and create loyalty; they will talk about it because you allowed them to create a meaningful experience for themselves. Author, brand expert, and Creative Warriors podcast guest Sally Hogshead tells a great story about letting customers create an experience.

Sally explains that there's a ride at Walt Disney World where you choose to enter in one of two lines: the green ticket line and the orange ticket line. The green ticket line is billed as the safer, more modest version of the ride. The orange ticket line is intended for only the bravest riders, the risk-takers, the ones willing to take on the full challenge of this ride. The orange ticket line was much longer. Obviously most people wanted the full experience. Why not, right? You're there, at Disney, ready to have fun! So of course Sally and her family chose the orange ticket line. The orange ticket line was abuzz. People excitedly took selfies holding their orange ticket. "Look at me, look at me! I'm in the orange ticket line." However, in the green ticket line, there was no excitement, no buzz. Few selfies were taken. "Yay, me. I'm in the kiddie line." I don't think so.

When the ride was over, Sally was curious about how different the experiences were. So she went in the green line also. The ride was virtually the same no matter which line you were in. What changed was the perception of the ride. Disney did a masterful job at letting people have their own experience. The choice between the green line and orange line alone was enough to allow riders to create their own experience.

Do you see something else from a branding perspective? As Sally told the story during our podcast interview, what stood out to me was the choice of color for each ticket. As colors, green conjures up neutrality and sameness, like "evergreen." Orange is an out-of-the-box color, unusual, vibrant, and exciting. So of course, green would be chosen for the mild version of the ride and orange for the exciting version. Even the simplest things become important in the secret language. Every little thing is a cue. Like an adjective in a sentence, it embellishes the language.

How can you set up the environment to let your customers have their own experience? What do you need to know about them? When I chose a downtown location for my photography business, I was aware of the power of experience. I didn't chose a location for my business directly on the main drag, what the locals called "the Avenue." Sure, that would have provided maximum exposure. But knowing the secret language of the ideal customer I wanted to attract, being in the typical location wasn't important. In fact, it seemed to me that being directly on "the Avenue" appealed more to visitors than to locals. I wanted to cater to town residents. So I chose a location on a secondary street, around the corner from "the Avenue," with the door facing a side parking lot, slightly tucked away.

The experience I wanted my customers to have was that they had discovered something special. My fifteen hundred square foot space was beautiful and perfectly appointed once you stepped inside. But there was no window to show my photos. Odd for a photographer, right? But I felt strongly that how my customers felt as they stumbled upon this hidden gem was far more important. The location allowed them to have an experience. I simply set up the situation. When people discover something, like a terrific bistro hidden in an ally, they are far more likely to tell others about their find. It's a rush to be the first to discover the next rock star, to be the first one in the know. My choice of location worked perfectly for twenty-two years.

The key is that you are setting up the environment or situation and allowing your customers to have the experience. Author and podcast guest Mike Michalowicz has one of the best websites I know. Check it out at www.MikeMichalowicz.com. It's incredibly well-branded and really captures Mike's playful personality. Mike is a friend and I can say, "This guy is authentic through and through." What you see is truly what you get. His website allows you, the visitor to the site, to have an experience. For example, there's an audio player near his name. Let's face it, Michalowicz is not the easiest name. As you keep tapping the audio player, Mike says every mispronunciation of his name possible. It goes on for a shockingly long time. He questions why you are still listening. He can't hear you say that you're laughing too hard to stop. What's the result of this experience? I have told countless others to check out his site! And this is not the only opportunity to party on Mike's site. There are dozens of photos of Mike doing all sorts of things. You never quite know what's coming so, of course, you keep looking. It's not often you can say you had a good time on someone's website.

Well, Mike Michalowicz certainly set up the environment for visitors to have a great time.

Mancrates.com is another website that fluently speaks the secret language of their testosterone-driven ideal customer. It offers gifts that come in a wooden crate along with a crowbar. For just an extra ten bucks, you can have crate and all encased in duct tape. Just watching some dude take forty-five minutes to get into his Man Crate is an experience. I give at least a few Man Crates every year for gifts.

Don't sell yourself short on this idea of setting up the environment for your customers to have an experience of their own. Be creative. Allow them to own the experience they have. Allowing people to take ownership of what they experience is love. It's sort of like not taking credit for the wonderful adults your children grow up to be. As parents, we set up the environment. But in the end, they own who they become. That's why allowing your customers to have an experience is part of the secret language of love.

COMMUNITIES THAT LAST AND EXPAND are built on more than just shared interests and experience. They are built on the fulfillment of secret desires. They are built on feeling understood in a profound way and experiencing something unique and personal. They are built on love. These are the things that create brand loyalty. I know you care about your customers. When you take the time to show them in ways I have described in this chapter, the community built around your business will naturally evolve and enhance not only your bottom line, but also your enjoyment in the daily work of your business.

⊛CH. 11
VALIDATION PARADOX

You CAN GET GREAT RESULTS in your business by applying the secret language strategies that you've learned in *LINGO*. I have no doubt. These are the exact strategies that I've used to build my own businesses as well as the businesses of coaching clients, and now that you are aware of them, you too can use them to create the business you want—one that feeds your soul, and your bank account.

But, my dear reader, there is another language that holds a key to your success: the language in your head. In this chapter, and in the two to follow, I will talk about the mindsets and practices that can free you from working hard, but not really getting ahead. Make no mistake—what's going on inside you will directly impact the outside results you will see.

I'll start by asking you a question: Did you feel different from the rest of your family growing up? Maybe even like the "black sheep?" Perhaps you felt you didn't fit in with the people around you? Not fitting in can be felt to varying degrees. It's a very common feeling amongst creative people. I'm not sure I could have felt more like a fish out of water. This feeling of being "different" that I have heard from so many and felt myself has always motivated me to understand why. Why do some of the most creative, innovative, and sensitive people feel out of place where they start in life?

Most importantly though, if we feel this way, how can we bring out the best in ourselves and reach our full potential? That's not a rhetorical question. I'm going to tell you how.

Before I do, let's first understand how it started. Feeling different can lead to feeling "less than." Many people I have worked with have shared that feeling different made them feel awkward or odd. They describe themselves as misfits. Yikes! That's painful. It also sets us up to not expect much of ourselves. It might cause others to not expect much from us. Expectation, by definition, is a pre-determined outcome. Whatever you expect you are capable of is likely to be as far as you'll stretch. Even if you think about exceeding your expectations, you've pre-determined what you're capable of. You've shut down the possibility that there's more in you than you might know.

The constant quest to prove and improve ourselves sets us up for what I call the Validation Paradox. In fact, we've been led to believe we have to find ourselves on our own— our authenticity, our why, and our purpose in life. Most of us have seen this as an inside job, something we have to do on our own. The paradox is that the best way to find ourselves is through others.

The African term Ubuntu loosely translates to "a person is a person through the affirmation of others" or sometimes, "I am I because of we." This term, Ubuntu, which has been traced to sources from the mid-nineteenth century, points out the need for others in order to find ourselves. We don't find ourselves, our truths, our purpose in life, our authenticity, even our why, on our own. In fact, it takes interconnectedness with others to find those qualities in ourselves. It takes others to see what we can't see in ourselves and to bring out more in us than we believe is possible. The only true way to go beyond your current expectation of yourself is to become what others believe you can be. This is why peer groups and masterminds are so valuable. It's the basis of the classic Jim Rohn quote, "You are the average of the five people you spend the most time with." If you want to rise to a higher level, hang out with people who are beyond your current state.

A sense of belonging is a human need. We seek community and to be part of something larger than ourselves. To reach our full potential, beyond what we can currently see, we have to let go of any feeling of being different or less than and find where we belong.

I recently sat at home enjoying crunchy snack food while watching Tony Awards. Most award recipients acknowledged their peers for "making them who they are." Sometimes how they grew up in a small Midwestern town and couldn't imagine they'd be receiving an award on the stage of the Tonys. Yet, here they were and it was "all because of you" they would tell their fellow actors and especially those closest to them. No matter where they started, what mattered and made all the difference in their lives was that they found where they belonged, which brought out their best. Recipient after recipient acknowledged the importance of their community in helping them be who they are and credited their community for getting them to where they are: on a stage, receiving an award.

Your ideal customers get you and probably see even more in you. Your ideal customers inspire you to deliver at an even higher level. This, I believe, is the true meaning of success breeds success.

I could never have reached the levels of success I did as a photographer had I not first found what sort of people I belonged with. Then I learned their secret language and built a business for them which spoke that secret language. It just so happened that where I belonged was amongst an affluent market. It actually had nothing to do with their affluence. It had everything to do with the values we shared. I felt as though I understood them. I "got them" and I suspected they would get me. They saw value in preserving special moments as a family grows. Heritage and handing something down from one generation to the next was a priority for them. They had the financial means to plan for the future and make sure everything's in order. All these are important values for a family portrait photographer.

I wholeheartedly felt that I found where I belonged, amongst a community of people who shared my values, who wanted what I had to offer. Quite frankly, people whom I understood better than I understood my family in many ways. Finding the affluent customer I could serve as a family portrait photographer gave meaning to feeling at home, to be at peace and amongst people who get what you're all about. I understand that business is business and maybe we shouldn't expect to feel this way. But when you find the ideal customers you are meant to serve, who see the best in you, you will find it easy to excel at levels you never imagined.

Can you see now how critically important it is to work with your ideal customers? It goes way beyond "nice to have." Working with the customers you "belong" with raises you up and gets you off the hamster wheel. Your expectations for yourself are fundamentally limited. Their expectations for you are not. It really is that simple.

Three things confirm you have found where you belong with your ideal customers:

1. Shared values
2. Mutual compassion
3. Ease of communication

When you share values with your ideal customers, you're on the same page, wavelength, or whatever you want to call it. I value long-term planning. It's a big part of my "why" as a family portrait photographer, to preserve family memories so they are available to enjoy in the future and even hand down.

Another high value for me is being responsible for loved ones. I'm the guy who pays bills before getting on a plane so I don't leave any trouble behind should the plane go down. You can imagine then, how comfortable it is for me to be around people who can afford to plan for the future and want everything in order. What are your most important life values? How does your line of work allow you to express your values? Who shares similar values?

I'm not sure how you can fully "get" someone without compassion. It's especially necessary to have compassion for your ideal customers if their lifestyle is different from your own. Without compassion and understanding for where they are coming from, you would always be at odds. Being at odds is certainly not speaking their secret language. Chances are you have considerable passion for them simply because of your choice of work.

I find most entrepreneurs are driven by solving a problem or keeping others from a pain they encountered. At the end of every interview on Creative Warriors, I ask my guests four Discovery Round questions. The intention of these questions is to peel back the curtain a bit and discover more than just their expertise. Now we want to know their thought processes and the tools they use. The first question is always the same: What drives you crazy? I ask that question because the purposeful work most people chose to do is in some way an attempt to prevent others from encountering something they've overcome or something they want to get over. This important question is asked at the end of a show to allow listeners the opportunity to connect all they've just heard about the guest's work and why it's important to them as way of correcting something that drives them crazy.

You know how some people are an absolute breeze to communicate with? You may have little or no history, but hit it off instantly. That ease of communication is the pinnacle of speaking a shared secret language. Many people describe feeling physically at ease when communication flows effortlessly, as it does when you are speaking your native language. Struggling to understand one another is exhausting! One of the promises of working with ideal customers is business becomes easier. Ease of communication is largely why. It's effortless, and there is less room for error and miscommunication.

◆

THE BENEFITS OF WORKING WITH your ideal customers, where you belong, are numerous. Yes, you've made your business more profitable. Sure, they are a pleasure to work with. But more than anything, you're working with people who bring out the best in you, people who validate who you are and what you're really capable of in business, and in life, people who see beyond the limitations you've inadvertently set for yourself and help you envision paths and possibilities you never dreamed possible.

⊛CH. 12
RECIPROCAL COMMUNICATION

Has there ever been something you worked really hard for that didn't work out? I can't imagine anyone can actually say "no" to that question. Have you ever looked back and thought, "Phew, it's a good thing that didn't work out"?

A couple of years ago I applied to speak at several TEDx events. It was always my dream to speak at a TEDx event. I was denied by every single one. Every. One. Was I devastated? Absolutely. But you know what, it's a good thing I wasn't accepted. My personal life was in shambles. I was in a volatile relationship with someone who derailed my focus every time I traveled. Had I been invited to speak at a TEDx event then, there was a really good chance I would have had to deal with issues at home as I was about to walk on stage. Sure, I would have plowed through, and maybe no one would have noticed because I'm a professional; I know how to pull it off. But I wouldn't have hit it out of the ballpark, and, at best, it would have been "good enough."

Since when do we entrepreneurs want "good enough"? Good enough isn't going to gain the recognition we need. Good enough is not what you want for your life, or you wouldn't be reading about speaking the secret language of your ideal customer. Clearly you want to have greater impact on people than "good enough." You are learning about LINGO so you can be more than good enough and have more than a superficial relationship with your ideal customer.

The bottom line with the TEDx events is, I wasn't ready. I thought I was at the time. For plans to work we need two-sided readiness. I was "ready" because I'm a trained and experienced speaker, but the goal, TEDx, wasn't ready for me. It wasn't the right time. So then, how do you make it your time to have the success you want? How can you assure that this is your time to get off the hamster wheel and start getting ahead?

First, I'll tell you want you can't do. You can't push your way through. Well, you can, the way I could have with the TEDx events at the time. But the ultimate goal of big-time recognition for my work would not have happened because my presentation would not have been exceptional enough to stand out. You know the expression, "you can't kid a kidder?" You can't kid your way to success. Somehow, someway, whatever goal it is that you want knows whether you're ready for it. If you're not, your goal will not be realized. If you and your goal are in sync, you have success. Incidentally, once I finished this book but before it was published, I was accepted as a speaker for TEDxLincolnSquare in New York City for 2018. Both I and my goal, were ready at the same time. My goal, to speak at a TEDx event, was ready to receive me.

This is what I call Reciprocal Communication: being in sync with your goals. It's about readiness, whether you're ready not just in ability, but also developmentally. Because if you are not developmentally ready, somehow the goal you seek knows. You can't kid a kidder.

Whenever you don't meet a goal, ask yourself whether you're really ready for it. I mean really ready. Or better yet, wonder what you can do to be developmentally ready for this next big level. If you've mastered your craft, whatever you offer, don't ask how you could do better. Ask how you can be more prepared to receive the rewards of your skills. If you're not ready to receive a goal— abundance, success, ideal customers—you will continue to work hard to push through and not get where you want to go.

Reciprocal Communication is actually quite simple. You can't force what you want. What you want has to "want" you back.

The goal of *LINGO* is for you to work only with your ideal customers by speaking their secret language. We're clear on that. You want ideal customers. But are you giving them good reason to want you back? The strategies that I've presented to you are meant to get you ready for your ideal customer. With empathy, compassion, non-judgment, openness, and genuine interest in others, you have cared enough to be ready for your ideal customer. But are you really ready to receive them? Are you ready to serve them?

In some of my trainings, I ask participants to make a list of the specific characteristics of their ideal customer. I want very specific details: they pay on time, they respect my work, they move quickly through my process, they use my technology, and so on. It's not terribly uncommon to do such an exercise. But I add a twist. I ask the participants to address the expectations of their ideal customer. Who do you need to be to deserve such ideal customers? If you expect them to pay on time, do you deliver on time? If you expect them to move easily through your process, do you make it as easy as possible to do business with you? Are you ready for your ideal customer? Are you who you need to be? LINGO teaches you how to be ready. Now you have to do the work. You have goals for your business and life. Maybe you can take it to the next level. Are you ready for the next level? My favorite quote is by author Jim Rohn who said, "Your level of success rarely exceeds your level personal development." As you increase your level of personal development, you create the space for your level of success to increase as well. To reach the new ceiling height you have set.

I've been observing this phenomenon my whole life. Recently I've been able to put words to it and I think it's time has come. People are looking for a better way to get to where they want to go in life than perpetually working hard. We value quality of life over quantity of hours spent. Paper maps took up half the car, you tried to find what you were looking for on the grid, and they never folded up the way they came out. Now we have GPS guiding us. We used to just push hard struggling with the maps. Now we know it doesn't have to be that way.

Let's look at some real life examples of Reciprocal Communication at play.

When I grew up in a rural town, one of the biggest sources of entertainment was bowling. I was on a couple leagues, and my extended family formed our own league. And I was really good! I had a high average and, of course, my own snazzy bowling ball and custom bowling shoes. As my skill as a bowler grew, I noticed sometimes the bowling ball slid seamlessly into the pocket for a strike. It was effortless, smooth and almost as if the pins were receiving the ball as opposed to being hit by the ball. Other times there seemed to be more struggle; I was throwing the ball with all my might which rarely, if ever, resulted in a strike.

Inevitably, despite my best effort to power my way through trying for a strike, one or two pins were left standing. I could tell the moment the ball left my fingers whether it felt right or not. I could tell whether everything was aligned for a strike or if I was left to hope for the best. But I couldn't put my finger on why this was or how to harness this awareness. Granted, I was barely a teenager.

I was at a cocktail party once and met a basketball player. I think he said he said he'd played in college. Not being a sports guy, I wasn't sure I had much to offer to the conversation. He explained he was a free-throw shooter. Relating the idea of hitting the pocket in bowling to free-throwing, our conversation quickly turned to what it feels like to free-throw.

I asked him, "When it's right, does it feel different?"

He said, "Yeah, you know the second the ball leaves your hands that it's going in. It's as if the hoop is taking the ball in."

Score! That's exactly the feeling I recall from bowling—the feeling that what you are aiming for is receiving what you're throwing instead of you hitting the target.

I once helped a coaching customer, Susan, get over a very rough spot in her business development process. In her frustration about not getting the results she wanted as quickly as she wanted them, she had become furious over the lack of help she was getting from other people. Susan had introduced her services to many people who praised her work but had not followed through on providing leads for her. She was feeling alone, disenchanted, and very frustrated.

As Susan explained her frustration to me, she would use words such as "those people," "they," and "no one can be trusted." I completely understood her frustration. It can be very discouraging when you are trying to start a business and you rely on the support and referrals of others.

After letting Susan release the pain she was feeling, I said to her, "You are talking about other people as if they are outside of you. As if it's you and 'them.' Do you understand that people won't step up and collaborate with you while they feel your separateness from them?"

She answered just as I expected she would. You see, Susan is a first-rate, class act and one of the most gracious people you'll ever meet. So of course she answered me by saying, "Oh no, I'm always very polite. I would never show my frustration."

"But what if they can sense it? What if it's unspoken?"

For many years, I studied Iyengar yoga under the watchful eye of one Mary Dunn. I attended classes with Mary every Thursday morning at The Iyengar Yoga Institute in New York City. Mary was an icon in the world of Iyengar yoga. I considered myself fortunate to be amongst her many adoring students. Tragically, Mary was struck by a rare type of cancer. Despite her treatments, Mary would still lead the classes whenever she was strong enough.

One day, after class, while rolling up mats and putting away wood blocks and belts used in the practice, I said to Mary, "How are you really doing?"

With absolute calmness and the same glimmer in her eye, she said, "I'm learning to walk toward life without being attached to the outcome." In one brief sentence, Mary expressed the fight to live that was inside her, while at the same time demonstrated she was at complete peace at not knowing what the outcome will be. She offered a lesson in softness, in not pushing toward what we're striving for. Mary lost her battle not long after.

When people are hoping to find the love of their lives, people often say, "It will happen when you're not looking for it" or, "Make yourself happy first, and happiness will find you." Consider the countless couples who try for years to conceive, hear "just relax and it will happen," decide to adopt, and then get pregnant.

In business, people talk about creating an impact and the money will follow. We've been hearing this message to not push, but haven't really fully understood the dynamic at play to understand the alternative. As goal-setting, hard-working entrepreneurs, we think "what choice do I have other than working hard to hit my goals?"

The alternative is to stop pushing so hard to hit our goals and instead, prepare ourselves, lessen the grip, and then initiate action. I've offered the strategies you can use to prepare yourself. Now lessen the grip, don't force, but get into action.

It's all too easy to think you can visualize and manifest things that will then happen on their own. But you need to initiate action without the hard push. Or as my yoga teacher, Mary Dunn, so wisely said, "Learning to walk toward life without being attached to the outcome." Walking toward is the action part. Letting go of the attachment to the outcome is the loosening of the grip. There's an old phrase that goes something like, "you can't receive with a clenched fist." A lessening of the grip is part of the process of Reciprocal Communication.

I don't believe success, or the love of your life, comes along because you're not focused on it. Success and whatever it is you seek comes along because you developed personally, prepared yourself, let your intention be known, loosened the grip, and that's why what you want shows up. You prepared first, stopped pushing, and allow it to happen. What you wanted showed up. This is Reciprocal Communication at work.

You want to set an intention, create a plan, do the groundwork, let it be known that's what you want by "putting it out there," initiate the action, and allow what you want to present itself. This is what so many of my coaching customers mean when they say they can feel that the success they want is right around the corner. As their coach, I can sense when they are right. It's because they've grown. Together we created a strategy, and they put in the work. They got the ball rolling by taking action, but they are not forcing it. They are allowing it. That's when I can see that it's real. Not that they don't need the change that is coming, especially if it means big financial rewards, but they are not coming from a place of desperation and force. They are not pushing. To stay with the bowling analogy, they are not throwing the bowling ball of life with all their might to knock down the pins. They have done all the right things to allow the pocket to receive the ball for a strike. Or the hoop to receive the basketball. Swoosh!

Being entrepreneurs, we are doers. That's such a positive trait! However, it can also cause us to push and inadvertently cause things to back up or push back, including our goals and all that we are working toward in the first place. That's the nature of resistance. Again, heed conventional wisdom, "What you resist, persists." If we resist loosening the grip, the resistance persists. We continue to work really hard, but don't get ahead as much as we'd like.

I interviewed author Sharon Spano on Creative Warriors. Sharon is the author of *The Pursuit of Time and Money: Step into Radical Abundance and Discover the Secret to a Meaningful Prosperous Life*. What Sharon does so well in her book is describe the pursuit of time and money not from a management perspective as is so commonly done, but from a personal development process. As with stages of personal development, we grow in our consciousness in our relationship to time and money.

As Sharon said to me in the interview, the idea of Reciprocal Communication is very high on the development scale toward a higher consciousness about abundance. Abundance is the collective feeling that comes from a successful business and fulfilled life; Reciprocal Communication is an opportunity for you to create the business and life you want from a place of higher consciousness. Plain and simple, it's deep in thought, but simple in its results. It feels like this is just the way life is meant to be. Less struggle. More ease. Better results.

Consider what you know now about Reciprocal Communication as your motivator to do the work to get ready for your ideal customer. Now you know being ready works because what you want wants you in return. That's what makes it all come together and helps you move ahead.

✱ CH. 13
SIX ESSENTIAL DAILY PRACTICES

WRITING A BOOK REQUIRES THAT you get very clear on what you want for your reader. I felt it was equally important to be clear on what I didn't want for you, my friend and reader. I didn't want *LINGO* to be yet another business book that provides you with strategies and action steps but doesn't help you actually break through and see tangible results.

What do most people say when asked, "What's your greatest obstacle?" The typical answer is, "I am." Most people acknowledge that they are their biggest obstacle. While I don't love the self-deprecating part of that, there is some truth to it. We are often working against ourselves. Applying all action without unblocking what's in your way is like pouring water into a channel that is dammed and wondering why there isn't any flow. This is what keeps us caught on the hamster wheel. We're not given an exit ramp. This chapter is your exit ramp. I wrote it so that as you apply the Secret Strategies, you also get out of your way and create a positive flow toward your goals.

That being said, you have to apply yourself. These mindsets and practices are not theoretical. You have to actually practice them. Otherwise you're caught in the same old loop. But I've been very intentional in keeping them simple. If it's too complicated or time consuming, you'll give up. I get it. Okay, let me point out the ultimate irony. In this chapter, you're going to learn how to change your mindset to unblock what's in your way. Then you're going to learn daily practices that create a positive flow and sustainable success. The result, if you apply yourself, will be more business and more success—which may mean less time. What happens then? Yup, you guessed it. Most people stop doing the practices that brought the success! The positive flow of success goes away and they think, "See, this stuff doesn't really work."

The hardest part is maintaining the right mindset and finding time for daily practices when they are working. It's a real test of your perseverance. It always reminds me of when you go to the doctor for an infection and you're prescribed an antibiotic. When you pick it up, the pharmacist always says, "Make sure you finish the entire bottle, even when you start feeling better." Why do they say that? Because, if you stop taking the antibiotic, you're more likely to have a relapse.

So stick with these mindsets and daily practices. They will reward you well. I've kept them simple and doable, even if you only have a few minutes each day.

Don't forget, I am with you. I'm also a hardworking entrepreneur and understand the challenge of sticking to these practices. But the rewards are worth it. A clear mindset, supportive daily practices, and the Secret Language Strategies are a winning combination. And I can rest easy knowing I was responsible and didn't just get you into action but also cleared the path to your success.

Without this preparation, you are likely to deflect some of the success that you have coming to you, which will keep you in the endless cycle of chasing what you're after. I don't want that for you. I want to see you succeed.

The suggested practices are divided into three ways of thinking and three actions. Try to incorporate all six into your life. Any practices you can add to these, such as meditation or yoga would be great. But, at a minimum, add these six practices into your life. I believe they will help break the cycle of needing to push too hard to reach your goals.

Also, don't give up if you skip practices. Just get back to it. The most important thing is to stick to it. Adjusting your mindset and employing these daily practices will, in time, create an inbound, unblocked flow that will result in you seeing the tangible results you are looking for. Ready? Let's do it.

BELIEVE THERE ARE FORCES WORKING ON YOUR BEHALF

FIRST, LET'S CHANGE THE WAY you think. Answer the following question: Do you believe there are forces working on your behalf?

Don't be quick to jump to a conclusion. When I first asked myself this question, being the eternally optimistic person I am, I was quick to jump to the conclusion that I absolutely believed the forces around me were working on my behalf. I was shocked when I really looked at the evidence of how I thought and how I behaved to realize that fundamentally, I did not believe the forces around me were working on my behalf. You may find yourself equally shocked when you look at your own life. I realized it was the root of why I worked so hard. Nothing was simply going to come along on its own, I thought. I'm the take charge, get things done guy.

How will you know whether your core belief is that forces are working on your behalf? Well, do you tend to think everything is up to you? Do you believe that if you want something done, you must do it yourself? Are you quick to take the blame when things go wrong and yet give credit to others when things go right?

You simply can't accomplish big things if you don't think there's something bigger than you working on your behalf. If you think it's all up to you, you will think you have the weight of the world on your shoulders. You will keep pushing, working harder and harder and not feeling like you're really getting anywhere, because if it's all up to you, you can never stop or it all falls apart. For hard working entrepreneurs, accustomed to getting stuff done, it can be very difficult to trust that it's not all up to them.

Trusting that there are forces working on your behalf is not like saying "everything happens for a reason," which is usually said when things go wrong. What we want is to trust that there are forces that want you to succeed. A wind at your back wants you to get where you want to go. Proof shows up in odd coincidences, moments of synchronicity, and even what appears to be dumb luck.

If you believe it's all up to you, then you are limited by what you think you are capable of. If you believe that anything is possible and there are forces working on your behalf, then you truly can see success beyond your expectations. Believing there are forces working on your behalf expands your mind and busts through any self-imposed glass ceiling. It allows you to think bigger than you are. That is essential to success.

The key lesson is trust. Trust that you have a safety net and that not only do people around you genuinely want you to succeed, there are also forces working on your behalf to assure that you succeed. It may not always look that way. It may seem it's all up to you. But if you want to succeed bigger than you can imagine, then you must count on something outside of yourself.

Start noticing when you feel the weight of the world on your shoulders. Shift your thoughts away from pressure of responsibility to trusting that somehow what you need will come along. It's similar to having a scarcity mindset. If you believe that there isn't enough or that your success is limited by what you make happen, then you are confining your success to a pre-established limited amount.

Success is not without effort or action steps. It's just not all effort and action steps. It's also trusting that there's a groundswell of support seeing to it that you will succeed. This may seem really ethereal. It's really just a mindset shift from living in fear and pushing to trust and receiving. I will admit, as an entrepreneur who's made every dollar on my own since the age of twenty, trusting that good things could happen without it being all of my own accord was a challenge. But I found as

I learned to trust, it felt like there was a collective power behind me. Maybe it's the ease of mind that enables you to think more clearly. Or the idea that you get more of what you focus on. It could be both, but it is certain that your success is not all up to you. So you may as well trust that the world wants you to succeed.

Realizing that it's not all up to you and trusting that there are forces working on your behalf is foundational to your success and life-changing. Live every day of your life believing this.

BE HIGHLY CONSCIOUS OF YOUR VIEWS OF OTHERS

IF YOU WANT TO BE successful, you have to be very careful not to have any negative opinions of others who are successful. This can stem from a deep-seated fear of being successful. I've had coaching customers say they are afraid they will become "too full of themselves." Or, they don't want to be "that person." I'm not sure they really know who "that person" is, they just have a very negative feeling about what happens to people who become successful.

Can you see how this would be a block to your success? How the fear of becoming too full of yourself could cause you to hold back and not achieve the level of success that you want? The fear is rooted in having negative opinions about successful people as if they are all full of themselves, boastful, conceited. Of course, who you are today does not have to be any different from who you are as a successful person. The success you can create will simply provide you with the lifestyle and freedom you may want or provide you with whatever else success means to you.

Also, be aware of any jealousy you might feel toward other people. Being genuinely happy for other people's accomplishments and success keeps you open to seeing the same in your own life. When you see someone acquire something you want or gain the recognition you want in your career, be happy for them. Recognize your desire and allow that to drive you toward your success. Say to yourself, "good for them, and someday I'll have that too."

Having negative feelings about people who have or accomplish what you want will create major mental blocks to your own success. Guaranteed. I refer to being highly conscious because you can acknowledge someone else's wins on the outside, through a fake smile, but be gritting your teeth on the inside and not even know it. Be honest with yourself. It will only serve yourself in the end. If you are harboring any negative views or jealousy about the success of others, it will block you from getting what you want. Clear yourself of any potential blocks to your success by paying very close attention to how you really feel about the success of others. Celebrate the wins of others and soon enough you'll be celebrating your own wins.

You must not hold any negative opinions about successful people or harbor any fear of who you will become as a successful person. Becoming highly conscious of your views of others is a major "unblocker" and a must to clear the way for your own success.

CONNECT WHAT'S IN COMMON

DO YOU EVER FEEL ALL over the place, as if you have too many interests and are going in too many directions? Connecting what's in common is the single most powerful realization I know of that can help you get clear on where you're going and committed to a direction to get there. Realizing what is in common in what appears to be a chaotic mess is the biggest jumpstart to get up and get going that I have ever witnessed in others and experienced myself.

The root of the problem is that the most creative minds that make for great entrepreneurs have likely been criticized for not being able to focus. As the creative mind wanders and develops a passion for many things, you're in a constant battle to rein it in because you've been led to believe you must focus. To manage this, you may compartmentalize your interests and passions and see them each as very different things.

In fact, many of them may be. However, in my experience, there is likely a common denominator in what inspires you and what you are passionate about.

I have interviewed countless guests on Creative Warriors who, on the surface, seem to have very diverse careers. However, when asked, they can identify a common interest that holds the whole body of their work together. It may not be obvious to everyone else, but it's clear to them. And really, all that matters is that it's clear to them, as it will be for you as well.

A great example of this is author Gretchen Rubin. Gretchen is most known for her book *The Happiness Project*, her podcast Happier, and all things around the topic of happy. But her earlier books, before *The Happiness Project*, include biographies of Winston Churchill, John F. Kennedy, and a book called *Power, Money, Fame, Sex*.

Collectively you might wonder what these topics have in common. Knowing that successful people can see the commonality in their work even if others can't, I suspected Gretchen knew exactly what was in common in her passions and interests. So I asked her about it. Her answer was human nature. She also added that, like a lot of people, she may not have seen the common denominator at first. But she followed her passions, and the common denominator presented itself. In fact, all her books are about human nature.

As discussed in Chapter 8, the New Niche is defined as what you are the go-to expert for. Then, paradoxically, once you have narrowed down what you are the go-to expert for, it expands what is possible to create around that expertise. It's similar to uncovering your common denominator. Once discovered, you realize you can create more around that common denominator and it will make sense. So, no longer are you living under the pressure of focusing on one thing or feeling guilty for being all over the place. As is the case with Gretchen Rubin, you can see now that all her books are in fact about human nature, whether it's about a person or a behavior.

I call the process by which I suggest you uncover your common denominator "taking the lid off" because the way to see what's in common is to first let loose what you may have been holding back. Make a list of all your passions and interests. No limitations. You should list as diverse a group of interests as possible. Then divide the list into six categories, any six categories you want. For example, these interests might be about communication. Those might be about transformation. Perhaps you have a group about science and logic. Choose any six categories that most, but not necessarily all, your passions and interests can fit into to. With this more manageable number, you can begin to see what's in common in these six categories. You're looking for a common thread. Feel free to get help from a friend or a coach. It might be easier for someone else to see what's in common in your interests.

The objective is for you to uncover the common denominator in what has made you feel like you were all over the place. This is liberating and will probably make you believe you get yourself at a level you hadn't before. This common denominator is not necessarily your purpose or "why." It's simply the bigger interest that weaves through what appeals to you. Why that appeals to you is a much bigger question. For the objective of this book and in interest of your success, for now I simply want you to be able to see what is in common in what appears to be diverse interests and passions.

When you can see what your passions have in common, you will work with more commitment, your mind will be clear, you'll know where you are going, and you'll be less susceptible to criticism. You will stay on track. This clarity leads to consistent effort every day, which leads to success.

Now, let's create success with specific actions:

CREATE AFFIRMATIONS

AFFIRMATIONS MAY BE SOMETHING YOU'VE heard about many times, maybe even tried a time or two and decided they didn't really do anything. I get it. So have I, as have more podcasts guests than I can count. Many very smart, "just want the facts," type of people have told me that they did not believe affirmations had any positive effect until they were proven otherwise. Despite initial resistance, they too had to surrender to the fact that affirmations do work.

I've heard many theories as to why and how they work. I look at it simply as a way to retrain the brain. You may be familiar with the idea that you get more of what you focus on. So sure, affirmations are a way of directing your focus. But I believe there's something even deeper at play that makes affirmations effective. It's the concept that you can only recognize what you already know. It's such an obvious concept that it can sound much more complicated than it is.

For example, if you've never seen a tennis ball, you would ask someone what it was the first time you came across one. When something is completely unfamiliar to us, we don't know what it is at all. Through the use of affirmations, you can make what you want far more familiar to you, thereby making it far more recognizable. You will literally begin to see much more frequently what you've been affirming. I believe that's why affirmations work.

What I love about affirmations is, it's a combination of art and science, ethereal and logical, left and right sides of the brain. While there is evidence of the neurological effects of affirmations, it's also helpful to know that they work without understanding how.

There are three important components of creating affirmations. The first is that you should affirm something specific. You don't want to affirm something vague such as, "I will be successful." Instead, affirm something specific that represents success to you, a specific amount of income per month, or something about the lifestyle of success, or perhaps a specific habit that will make you more successful.

Secondly, it must be affirmative. Sounds obvious, right? But you might be surprised. You want your affirmation to be definitive, confident, and clear. A while back I was working on an affirmation that initially was, "I will be loved and acknowledged by a world that I love and acknowledge." I was craving more recognition for the work I was doing and understood that it's not a one-way street. In order to be loved and acknowledged, I had to love and acknowledge the world around me. It sounded great, and I was pleased with my affirmation, which I would repeat over and over again in my head.

One day, a few weeks into this affirmation, I realized it wasn't very affirmative at all! I was saying, "I will be loved and acknowledged…" "I will" as in someday, hopefully, maybe. Not affirmative, confident, and clear at all. So I changed it to, "I am loved and acknowledged by a world that I love and acknowledge." Be sure your affirmation is affirmative, that you say it with confidence, and that it's so clear it rolls off your tongue—even if you're only repeating it in your own head.

Lastly, you must repeat your affirmation. There are mixed opinions on how often or how many times an affirmation should be repeated to be effective. Because these are daily practices and sticking with the practices is more important than reaching a goal, my suggestion is to do what works for you. If repeating an affirmation for five minutes at the end of a meditation practice works for you, then great! If repeating your affirmation like a tape running in the background of your mind throughout the day works for you, then go for it.

I've made repeating an affirmation part of my morning dog-walking routine. To the rest of the world it looks like I'm walking my dogs. For me, it's a forty-five-minute opportunity to repeat my affirmation in five-minute spurts. Multi-tasking at its best. It's most important that the affirmation be repeated often.

As for how long you should stick with an affirmation, my advice is: beyond when you see results. This is where I think many people fall apart with affirmations. They either don't stick with it long enough to see results or they stop using the affirmation as soon as they see results. People often affirm something about success, let's say more customers, and as soon as success comes their way, they are too busy to keep up with the affirmation. They end up where they started, and claim affirmations don't work. My suggestion is to stick with an affirmation for as long as it takes to see results. Keep with it until what you were affirming is fully integrated. Then feel free to move on to another affirmation, maybe one about being stress-free and relaxed because of all the newfound success from your previous affirmation.

"WHAT'S GOING RIGHT" JOURNAL

THIS IS A DAILY PRACTICE I made up and the one that has had the greatest positive effect on my life and business. It started with struggling to maintain a gratitude journal. Don't get me wrong. Gratitude journals are fantastic and helpful for many people. For me though, a gratitude journal just wasn't enough. It was too vague and not actionable enough. If you've ever felt that way, then the What's Going Right Journal may be a perfect fit for you.

The biggest challenge I had with gratitude journals is that I'm grateful for everything. I'm grateful I wake up in the morning. I'm grateful for my health. I'm grateful my kids are well. I'm grateful for blue skies. If you're really grateful, where does it end? With no boundaries, I found it impossible to maintain interest in journaling about what I was grateful for. Also, while I could see how gratefulness brought more awareness about what I had in my life to be grateful for, I didn't see how it would bring more into my life. It helped me appreciate what I had, but didn't create more of the prosperity I desired. I wanted something more.

So I created a What's Going Right Journal. The idea is to journal about what's going right in your life. You know how you can hear ten compliments and one insult and all you can think about is the insult? Or "constructive criticism." That's because as a matter of survival, our brains are wired for survival. We automatically focus on anything that is a threat to us. It may not be the threat of a lion entering our cave, but it might be a threat to our confidence or self-worth or a threat to our feeling of satisfaction in a job well done. The negative by far outshines the positive. So as we go about our days, we are likely to become much more aware of what's not going right. The challenges, obstacles, and technical mishaps. We close a deal and quickly move on and take on the next challenge, nearly overlooking the good event.

The What's Going Right Journal reverses that. It brings out the positive. It forces you to take note of what's going right in your life. It's not always easy to see what's going right! And that's proof right there how much you need a What's Going Right Journal! Because it can be a challenge to see what's going right, I journal in two steps. You don't have to do it this way, but it works for me and allows the unconscious brain, the part of my brain that has a tendency to overlook the positive, to come alive.

Shortly after I wake up in the morning, I sit with my journal and think about what's going right. It may be a surge of interest in my coaching services. It may be a new customer. It may be positive feedback on an article or the podcast. I find this can be a bit of a struggle at first. All the things going right, especially the small ones, can be buried. So once I get stuck, I don't force it and put down my journal. Then I walk my dogs and repeat my affirmation. As my brain begins to fully awaken, and I take in the beautiful environment of life on the beach that I am so grateful for, the numerous things that are going right come pouring to mind.

As you can see, gratefulness can be a key that unlocks the awareness of what's going right, but it's journaling the specifics of what's going right that becomes more actionable. It's more actionable because the practice of the What's Going Right Journal creates a positive flow. As with affirmations, you get more of what you focus on and you can only recognize what you already know. As you begin to notice and journal about what's going right, guess what happens? You start seeing more of what's going right! And that means there's more of what's going right in your life.

The What's Going Right Journal creates a tangible, positive flow like nothing else I've seen. And because it's specific and requires thought, I believe it's easier to stick with over the long haul than many other journaling processes. A What's Going Right Journal is a lifelong practice.

What could be better than seeing more of what's going right in your life and business?

PRODUCTIVITY BEGINS THE NIGHT BEFORE

WITH ALL THE DIFFERENT HATS you wear as an entrepreneur, you need to be highly productive. It should be pretty clear to you by now that, while being successful requires a lot of prep work, such as learning the secret language of your ideal customer, it also takes action. You must get into action and make the best use of your time. As an entrepreneur, there are never enough hours in the day. Yet, the whole point of speaking the secret language of your ideal customer and only working with your ideal customers is not working every hour of your life. Your time is valuable. Your life hours cannot be replaced. There is simply no time to waste, because you have a contribution to make and there's no time to waste getting the best of you out in the world.

As an entrepreneur, there's a good chance your business relies significantly if not entirely, on you. If something happened to you, would your business exist? Could it go on? I'm not trying to be morbid, but simply to point out that your well-being and productivity is crucial to the success of your business. To be successful, get as much done, in as efficient a manner as possible, toward the direction that will have the greatest impact.

My goal every day is to work on three things that will most move the needle. Everyday. It's easy to get caught up in to-do lists, admin responsibilities, and urgent matters and not devote enough energy toward the things that will have the greatest impact on your goals. This just continues to contribute to that feeling of being a hamster on the wheel, running fast but not really getting anywhere. So how do we break the cycle of a crazy amount of activity but not getting ahead?

A productive day begins the night before. Look at the night before as the on-ramp to your day to come, so you don't have to go from zero to sixty at the crack of dawn. Instead of looking at your day as beginning at seven a.m. or whenever you get up, look at the morning as a continuation of the night before, leading to a productive day.

There are several reasons why this is important. First, to be your most productive, you need to be rested. I know, I know. I'm as guilty as anyone of trying to slide by on as little sleep as possible. But you know you aren't at your best when you're tired. Driving tired has been compared to driving while intoxicated. That says all you need to about your inability to be at your best and sharp when you're tired. So the first step to having a productive day is to go to sleep at a time that allows you to get the sleep you need, the amount of sleep you need to feel fully rested.

Make sure your sleep is also as productive as possible. Many people struggle with sleeping well. I can't promise to solve the issue, but as someone who sleeps as if he's in a coma, let me share some of my sleep practices that I believe have contributed to sleeping so soundly. Going to bed at around the same time and for roughly the same number of hours is helpful. I think it's a good practice to set an alarm for when you need to go to sleep rather than for when you need to wake up—or maybe both. But knowing when it's time to call it quits and get to sleep is important.

Because sleep is imperative to a productive day, think of sleep and your bed as sacred. I hate to break it to you, but that means no electronic devices in the bed. By this I mean no smartphones, tablets, and laptops. Back lit screens that emit blue light have been proven to suppress melatonin, the sleep hormone, and mess with your body's natural circadian rhythm, to say nothing of the content that could weigh on your mind and keep you awake. All it takes is one Facebook post about a competitor's latest win to keep you up for hours stewing in envy. Why take the risk?

Consider your bed the boundary for your communication to the outer world. Don't allow it. Try not to watch TV in bed. Read only if it's relaxing or makes you sleepy. Consider going to bed your prep time for a productive day. Hold it as sacred time. Getting into bed should be a cue that it's time to rest. If you make a clear distinction that this is sleep time, perhaps the quality of your sleep will improve. If not, allow extra time in bed to make up for restless nights.

Podcast guest John O'Leary mentioned to me that every night before he goes to sleep, he journals on the question, "What more can I do to ensure tomorrow is even better than today?" Now that we got sleep out of the way, a productive day actually begins before that. You might want to glance at your schedule and what needs to get done the next day before getting into bed. By glance, I mean take a soft look so you can prepare yourself by thinking, "I've got this." Not to stress about it, or put anything on your mind, this glance is just so you know what's ahead before going to sleep. When you do this, you wake up more prepared for the day.

I'm also a believer in the subconscious brain's ability to process and even solve real problems. It turns out, there is something to the old adage to "sleep on it." Present your brain with a problem or your desire for an idea or solution and let your subconscious brain work on it. You just might wake up with what you need, or the idea or solution may pop into your head later on, probably while you're showering or driving to work.

This leads us to the power of thoughts the night before as a means for productivity. Hal Elrod in his book *Miracle Morning* explains that a body of evidence suggests that, if you go to sleep with the thought that you going to wake up tired, you are more likely to wake up tired, as opposed to thinking you'll wake up feeling rested even if you don't get enough sleep. Why not feed the next day with the most positive thoughts possible the night before?

As you lay still for a few minutes, know that you've got this. The next day is yours to own. You're going to kill it and accomplish all that you set out to do. There will be a positive flow coming toward you, and you are within reach of all that you set out to accomplish. Set the thoughts the night before for the optimal way that you want to wake up in the morning and spend the rest of your day being pumped and highly productive.

Productivity does start the night before. The next morning is the continuation of the stage you set. The morning after is the on-ramp of the highly productive day ahead of you.

By INTEGRATING THE THREE MINDSET shifts, you unblock any potential thought processes that could keep your success away. The three action steps create a positive flow. Like the bread to a sandwich or the cookie to an Oreo, these mindsets and practices protect the good stuff. As you apply the strategies you've learned in *LINGO*, you've protected and far more ensured your success with these practices. Unblock, do the work, and create a positive flow for more. That's the formula for success. It's remarkably simple, really. Typically, we work really hard but our mindsets get in the way. Or, if we've done the unblocking work, we work really hard but it's not accumulating because we haven't created a positive flow. Those three areas need to work in harmony—clear the path, put in the effort, an open channel to receive.

CONCLUSION

I WAS NEVER THE POPULAR kid. In fact, I was the kid teachers forgot was in the room. I was almost always the last one chosen for the kickball teams because I hid in the back of the line. No one noticed I was there. I'd like to say that changed as an adult, but not always. I was once out to dinner with a friend, and the waitress walked up to the table and asked my dining partner how his meal was. She walked away without even acknowledging I was at the table. My meal was good, too, but it's nice to be asked. I get insulted when I use public bathrooms and the motion detector doesn't know I'm there to turn the faucet on so that I can wash my hands. I start waving like a fool. So being noticed right away hasn't proven to be my thing. Except in business.

When I started my photography business in my hometown, barely anyone noticed. Within one year of my first visit to Bergdorf Goodman, I went from being overlooked to being overbooked. Within just a few years, I had an eight-week waiting list. Today, I lead other Creative Warriors to their own success. All because of the Secret Language Strategies I've shared with you in *LINGO*.

Now it's your turn. You can do this. You, too, can take your business from being overlooked to overbooked, or whatever version of that suits your business. You can be the brand that people are so devoted to that they are less focused on price and more interested in how doing business with you makes them feel. You can, and will, be the business that becomes known for your area of expertise.

But, you have to do the work. I interviewed Vincent Pugliese, author of *Freelance to Freedom*, for Creative Warriors. He mentioned something in his book I couldn't wait for the opportunity to throw into our conversation.

"Vincent," I said, "let's talk about your big butt."

Okay, I meant "but" and I knew he'd know what I was talking about. You see, in Freelance to Freedom, he mentions that we all have a big but, the big but that we use as an excuse, the big but that, well, is a pain in the butt. It's the excuse or excuses we use to not do what we know is probably the best thing for us to do.

So let me see if I can name a few of your big buts as to why you might not apply what you've learned in *LINGO*:

This will only work with high-end customers.

Wrong! The entire point of the secret language is that every market has a secret language. High-end, low-end and everything in between. Teenagers, left-handed people, corporate folks, people who dye their hair pink. It doesn't matter. What matters is if you're willing to understand them.

I don't have the money.

Terrific! This is the cheapest education you'll ever get! No business school is going to teach you how to understand and speak the secret language of your ideal customers! It costs nothing to have empathy, compassion, and be willing to do the work to walk in their shoes. It costs nothing to want to deeply "get" people.

It seems like a lot of work.

So, how is working hard but hardly getting ahead working for you? Whether you're a startup or have been in business for decades, there's no better time to align your business with your ideal customers than now. A little work upfront will save you years of struggle later on. Is it worth it to make your business irresistible? I'll let you decide.

I don't know how to start.

Starting is key. Start today. Start by going where your ideal customer already is, online and offline. Start by looking at brands your ideal customer is already interacting with. Or, start by opening your heart to caring and your mind to what's possible. But you must start.

What's your big but? Whatever it is, get it out of your way, because a whole new possibility lies before you: getting paid what you're worth, feeling valued for what you do, and working with customers who are a joy to work with. It's a way of being in business that, quite frankly, will probably be more comfortable to you because it's based on human interaction, not business transaction.

Whenever I hear someone say, "I'm not good at the business side," I always want to say, "Maybe it's because you haven't been in business in a way that's natural for you." Call me naive. You won't be the first. But I believe people, our customers, are innately good and want meaningful relationships, even with businesses and brands. Imagine what's possible when you show up wanting to connect on a deeper, more meaningful way with your customers, and it's what they want too. Still worried about whether people will pay for that? I wouldn't be. Making people feel like you get them will make your business irresistible.

I'm with you. Three simple words I have held with me every moment of writing *LINGO*. I'm with you because I do get you. Perhaps, by now, you feel you get me too. We're in this thing called entrepreneurship together. I call us Creative Warriors, the brave souls creating stuff and transforming people's lives. We're on the front line of creating change in the world with creative solutions, innovative products, and passionate desire to make a difference.

I'm thrilled, and you should be too, that we live in a time when people demand a more personal connection than ever before to do business with us. We can do this, and perhaps the big guys can't, at least not as quickly, because big business is not as agile as we Creative Warriors are. This demand to be treated like an individual causes us to up our game and meet a new, higher standard. Cursory relationships in business will no longer be enough. Just meeting expectations will cause you to be overlooked. Not understanding those you are building your business for will cause you to miss the mark. And you can, and will be, substantially rewarded for your willingness to "get" your ideal customers by speaking their secret language.

It's for this reason I end every Creative Warriors podcast episode with this message:

Create, serve, and be prosperous.

Because you do deserve to create what you're passionate about and to serve by speaking the secret language which will lead to prosperous results. It's your turn now.

✱APPENDIX

EXERCISES

◆

WHO WILL LOVE THAT?

IN CHAPTER TWO, RATHER THAN simply identifying your ideal customers, you also explored who you are and what you have to offer in order to determine who would love that about you. What follows is a series of questions I posed in the chapter. Set aside time to get to clarify who you are and whom you want to serve. Remember, your ideal customers are waiting for you to show up!

1. What are your innate characteristics—your preferences, quirks, and other personality traits that make you you?
2. What are your top three life values—the values you are willing to fight for?
3. What do you do, create or offer? And why is what you're offering so important to you that you're willing to play the game day after day? What value is it fulfilling or what transformation is it creating that makes it so important to you?
4. If your ideal customer reviewed your business, product, or service, what are the top three things you want every one of your ideal customers to say? What are three things you want to excel at that are most important to your ideal customer.
5. What price point do you serve?
6. Considering all of the above, who would love that? Who are the people who would love you for who you are, share similar values, want what you offer, have a priority for your unique strength, and can afford you? Be as specific as possible.

EXPLORATORY MISSIONS

IN CHAPTER ONE, I SHARED the story of my discovery trip to Bergdorf Goodman in search of clues about the affluent clients I wanted to work with. It was the beginning of my journey to learning the secret language of my ideal customers. Learning your ideal customer's secret language requires multiple exploratory missions—to brick-and-mortar establishments, neighborhoods, and public spaces; to virtual and online locations; and in the things your ideal customer's read, listen to, and enjoy.

When you go to a store or restaurant your ideal customer might love, take in all the details and write them down. Here are some questions to get you started:

1. What does the physical environment look like?
2. How would you describe the atmosphere? Is it warm and friendly or bright and fast-moving?
3. What are the common colors, scents, and sounds? Is it loud or quiet?
4. Are there long lines or do people sit and wait to be served?
5. Is the staff wearing uniforms?
6. Notice how the customers and salespeople behave and interact. What expectations are being met?
7. What does it feel like?
8. What is the jargon used by staff?
9. What is the etiquette?
10. At the store, are the brands your ideal customers are drawn to high-volume chains or custom-oriented?

11. What's the price point? Are the brands high-end, low-end, or somewhere in between? Are the prices visible or hidden?

12. What kind of music is playing, if any?

13. Is there enough staff to give individual assistance or are the customers pretty much on their own?

Understanding your ideal customer's perspective requires other research as well. Here's a list of questions to get you started:

14. What magazines or blogs do they read?

15. What charities do they support?

16. What common experiences do they share?

17. What social events do they attend?

18. What holidays do they observe?

19. What behaviors do they share?

20. What are their top values?

LEARN FROM OTHER BRANDS

I'M A HUGE FAN OF cross-industry innovation. You can learn from other industries and businesses that are completely different than your own. Cross-industry innovation offers you an opportunity to take a fresh look at your business, give it a twist, and stand out from others in your industry.

You don't have to copy what other brands have done or take ideas from their websites to apply to your website. Instead, "mash up" what you've learned about these other brands from all their assets, online and offline, and apply those ideas to your website.

As you research other brands, take note of the following:

1. Are the brands your customers like contemporary or traditional?
2. How do familiar brands present their merchandise in the store as well as online?
3. Is the presentation cluttered or simple?
4. Do you get a sense of the price point of these familiar brands?
5. Are they accessible for everybody, exclusive, or right for a particular market?
6. Is there focus on a particular age bracket or gender?
7. What about colors and tones?

♦

WHAT IS YOUR BRAND STYLE?

IN CHAPTER 5, WE EXPLORED the secret language of style, the language of how things look. Speaking the secret language of style is creating recognition, having your ideal customers qualify themselves because your style resonates for them, and helping them make a quick decision.

Recall that there are three components to brand style: personality, voice, and price point. In Chapter 5, I shared a series of exploratory questions to help you identify your style and ensure that it speaks to your ideal customer:

1. What is the personality of your brand? Humorous, classic, professional, casual? I suggest starting with five words that capture the essence of the personality you want to portray.
2. Do these five personality traits complement one another and make for a compelling brand? If they were the five personality traits of a person, would you be compelled to want to know more about this person? Does he or she seem like someone who has depth and is likeable? How authentic are these five personality traits to you?
3. What does the voice of your brand look like? If you were to direct it as a scene in a play, how would it go?
4. Consider the image your brand projects. Does the style you portray seem like your actual price point? If you were your customer, based on what you saw, would you be surprised by your prices? Would you be shocked it cost so much more than you expected? Or would you think it's a bargain because you expected it to be much more?

◆

QUESTIONS TO HELP YOU IDENTIFY YOUR SECRET LANGUAGE OF PRICING

I'M CONFIDENT THAT UNDERSTANDING THE secret language of pricing and positioning myself correctly was the number one reason for my success. There's a good chance pricing will make or break your business too. At the end of Chapter 6, I shared a few questions to help you identify your ideal customer's lingo around pricing. Here's that list again:

1. Do your ideal customers live like you, or are they wealthier or not as wealthy as you?
2. If you're buying something for a hobby or interest that you are passionate about, say a bicycle, handbag, or musical instrument, what's the top of the range of what you're willing to spend?
3. Considering your answers, what might be the range your ideal customer would be willing to spend on what you offer?
4. List three words to describe the perception you want people to have about your business.
5. Which of the following gives the feeling you want people to have of your business?
   a. 35
   b. $35
   c. $35.00
   d. $34.99

◆

SELF-IDENTIFYING QUESTIONS

IN CHAPTER 7, WE EXPLORED the secret language of words. As part of that chapter, I shared the power of self-identifying questions. These are questions you will pose in your marketing that are compelling to the audience you want to attract, while probably everyone else will pass them by. Self-identifying questions have the power to stop someone in their tracks, get their attention, and immediately make them feel like you get them.

This is the process for coming up with self-identifying questions:

1. Know who your ideal customer is.
2. Understand their perspective. What are they going through? What are they feeling?
3. What are they thinking about?
4. What question finishes the thought and offers a solution?
5. Once you have several self-identifying questions, test them on your ideal customer.
6. Narrow down your questions to the most powerful few.

◆

CREATE A STAND OUT STATEMENT

As PART OF THE SECRET language of words, I shared with you the power of creating a Stand Out Statement. This statement lets the world know what you stand for, who you stand with, and how you to stand out. It is concise and to the point, made up of just three to seven words.

Creating your Stand Out Statement is a process, a journey, if you will. So we start with what I call a Quest Statement. With the Quest Statement, you will determine the four essential components of the Stand Out Statement:

1. Your unique expertise
2. The ideal customer
3. Emotions of their challenge
4. The solution you provide

The Quest Statement is a fill-in-the-blanks format. Fill in the blanks in the following sentence:

As the go-to expert on [your unique expertise], I help [ideal customers] who feel [emotions of their challenge] so that [the solution you provide].

With your Quest Statement complete, you can start working on your Stand Out Statement. You do this by capturing the entire essence of your Quest Statement in three to seven words. The essence. The feeling. The heart of the matter.

My Quest Statement:

As the go-to expert on speaking the secret language, I help uncommon entrepreneurs who feel frustrated they are wasting their time not getting paid what they're worth so that they can attract and keep their ideal customers and turn their businesses around.

Became this Stand Out Statement:

Freedom Fighter for the Uncommon Entrepreneur

ACKNOWLEDGMENTS

RELATIVELY SPEAKING, A BOOK DOESN'T take that long to write. It's all the experiences, the trials and tribulations, the relationships, and the support that take a lifetime to accumulate—and, for a number of individuals, a lifetime to show my appreciation.

I first want to thank my editor, Anjanette Harper. I don't know how common it is that an author thanks their editor first. But AJ, as I call her, is no common editor. If there's one person I can truly say I would never have been able write this book without, it's AJ.

I'd like to thank my kids, Connor, Clare, and Lilly. No words can ever express my love and respect for these three individuals. It's a special thing when you can say your kids are simply great people. My mom has ridden along on the crazy journey of my life every step of the way, most of the time having no idea where we're headed, but accepting me for who I am anyway. I'd like to thank the dearest friends anyone could ever ask for. If they weren't loved by so many, I'd say one rarely has a chance in life to have such great friends as I have in Nancy and Roger Pellissier. A new friend walked into my life just as I was beginning this book and became a fast and forever friend, Denise Jacobs. It's never a bad thing to have as a friend someone who wrote a book called *Banish Your Inner Critic* when you're writing a book of your own.

Amy and Michael Port, what can I say? Michael came up with the name *LINGO* and nailed it. Amy's words of wisdom have been a shining light so many times when I couldn't see, I don't even know where to begin. I'd like to thank Naomi Niles for her stellar design work on the cover and the entire team at Interview Valet for their support on getting all my podcast interviews set up. I'm not sure whether to thank my podcast team for their patience or their effort, I suppose both. Thanks, Colin, Enid, and Cheryl.

A huge amount of gratitude goes out to all my podcast guests. I've learned a tremendous amount from each and every one of you, as well as all the gracious hosts who have had me as a guest on their show. I have thirty-three years of photography clients to thank for bringing out the best in me and helping me achieve levels of success and personal growth I never thought would be possible. I've met amazing people in Masterminds and trainings, too many to mention, but a few include Amy Rader, Tamsen Webster, Tom Webster, Joey Coleman, Andrew Davis, Laura Belgray, Melanie Spring, David Burkus, Melissa Smith, Kris Marsh, David Wells, and James Taylor. There's a bit of each of you in this book. Dorie Clark, your guidance, generosity, and friendship have meant the world to me. I'd like to thank my CTI Leadership tribe for seeing more in me than I was prepared to see at the time and then lending support to help me get there.

A tremendous amount of gratitude and respect goes out to the entire Creative Warriors community. To the podcast listeners, members of Creative Warriors Unite, coaching clients, attendees at speeches, readers, and all of you brave souls bettering the world with your work and message, namaste. I truly honor the light in you. It is humbling to be in your presence.

Lastly, I thank Lawrence. You may have come along and into my life midway through the writing of the book, but your impact has been a lifetime's worth.

ABOUT THE AUTHOR

JEFFREY SHAW HAS ALWAYS BEEN an entrepreneur. At the age of fourteen, barely able to see over the steering wheel, he would use his mother's car to sell eggs door-to-door. Keenly aware of marketing strategies even then, he made his eggs available on Saturdays in anticipation of Sunday morning breakfast. The eggs sold for $1.25 a dozen, which was a premium price in 1978. Since it wasn't just about the eggs but also about the relationship, Jeffrey felt the higher price was justified.

He took up photography as a hobby, initially fascinated by the chemical interaction in the darkroom and the ability to bring a latent image to life. By the age of twenty, Jeffrey graduated with the Best Portfolio Award and was selected to speak at graduation as student representative of The Hallmark Institute of Photography.

One of the most sought-after portrait photographers in the US, Jeffrey photographed the families of such notables as sports stars Tom Seaver and Pat Riley, news anchor David Bloom, supermodel Stephanie Seymour, and C-Suite executives from Twitter, Anheuser Busch, and 3M, as well as Wall Street leaders too many to mention. His portraits have appeared on the *Oprah Winfrey Show*, in *People* magazine, *O, the Oprah Magazine*, CBS News, and more.

Having been a photographer for more than three decades, Jeffrey realizes a keen eye isn't just for what one sees, but also for what one senses. To be able to sense the needs of others as well as trends in business keeps you a step ahead. Jeffrey Shaw, a.k.a. *The Lingo Guy*, uses this honed intuition to teach entrepreneurs how to attract their ideal customers by speaking their Secret Language.

Today, Jeffrey is host of the popular business podcast *Creative Warriors*, a featured storyteller on *The Moth*, and a nationally acclaimed keynote speaker on the topics of marketing, branding, customer relations, and sales. Jeffrey's first book, *LINGO: Discover Your Ideal Customer's Secret Language and Make Your Business Irresistible*, is the culmination of a lifetime of entrepreneurship.

Jeffrey is the father of three adult children and resides with his two dogs in Miami Beach, Florida. He claims the dogs are more work than the kids ever were.

RESOURCES

PLEASE CONNECT ON SOCIAL MEDIA!

Twitter: https://twitter.com/jeffreyshaw1
Facebook: Creative Warriors Unite Group at http://joinwarriors.com
Instagram: https://www.instagram.com/jeffreyshaw/

LISTEN TO CREATIVE WARRIORS PODCAST!

iTunes: http://creativewarriorsunite.com/itunes
Google Play: http://creativewarriorsunite.com/google
Creative Warriors website: http://creativewarriorsunite.com

INQUIRE ABOUT SPEAKING

JEFFREY IS AVAILABLE FOR KEYNOTES and breakout sessions. "Make Your Business Irresistible: The Secret Language Strategy" is his signature keynote that will inspire and provide actionable steps. Inquire about keynotes and presentations at http://jeffreyshaw.com/speaking.

ADDITIONAL SUPPORT

The FREE LINGO Media Kit
Contains an infographic of the 5-Step Secret Language Strategy, a free chapter of LINGO, and a free audio chapter with additional

content and sound effects. Grab your FREE LINGO Media Kit at http://lingomediakit.com.

LINGO Coaching

Make your business irresistible and only work with your ideal customers with Jeffrey's help! Programs available are: one-to-one coaching, group workshops, and an online course. For more information, go to http://lingocoaching.com.

Business Coaching: One-to-One and Group

Various business coaching options are available for complete support of your business covering branding, marketing, sales, pricing, enrolling, and customer service. Inquire here: http://jeffreyshaw.com/coaching